# Losing *the* Plot

*Andrew McIndoe*

**AA**

Published by AA Publishing, a trading
name of AA Media Ltd, whose registered
office is Fanum House, Basing View,
Basingstoke, Hampshire RG21 4EA.
Registered number 06112600

Packaged for AA Media Ltd by OutHouse
Winchester, Hampshire SO22 5DS

For OutHouse:
Managing editor  Sue Gordon
Art editor  Robin Whitecross
Editor  Lesley Riley
Proofreader  Lindsey Brown
Indexer  June Wilkins

First published in the UK in 2009

Text copyright © Andrew McIndoe 2009

Andrew McIndoe has asserted his right
to be identified as author of this work in
accordance with the Copyright, Designs
and Patents Act, 1988.

A CIP catalogue record for this book is
available from the British Library.

ISBN 978 0 7495 6158 1
ISBN 978 0 7495 6272 4

Reproduction and colour separation by
MRM Graphics Ltd
Printed and bound by Printer Trento, Italy

A03704

**Previous page**: *Hydrangea serrata*
'Bluebird'. **Opposite**: *Hosta* 'Patriot'.

# Contents

# Gardening for the time of your life

**Top**: Roses and perennials quickly fill the beds: lovely, but not low maintenance. **Centre**: *Cephalaria gigantea*, a statuesque perennial reaching 2m (6ft) or more. **Above**: *Vitis coignetiae*, a rampant climber with wonderful autumn colour.

Often our first garden is influenced by child-hood memories and ideals of what a garden is all about. Even the trendiest new garden owner cannot help but desire roses, honeysuckle round the door, an herbaceous border, a meadow of wildflowers and a vegetable plot brimming with produce, regardless of the practicality of fitting them into the space, or the feasibility of maintaining them.

Having been involved with plants and gardening all my life, my first garden was a release from years of the frustration of living in rented property and a flat. Despite the modest size of my new-build garden, I had to have every shrub and climbing rose I had ever wanted. *Cephalaria gigantea* erupted from the gravel, and *Vitis coignetiae* smothered the nearby indigenous planting that had been driven into the ground unceremoniously by the departing developers. Access to the front door was hindered by a hedge of *Rosa* 'Felicia' underplanted with copious alchemilla

and nepeta. Needless to say, the garden was overfilled after a couple of seasons, but I had no regrets; it had satisfied my desires within the timescale I had in mind.

When we moved on to our cottage in the country I lamented the loss of my roses, but took little with me apart from a few roots of forget-me-not, some wild violets, a few *Viola cornuta*, some honesty seedlings and my pots. The plants were all descendants of those in my garden when I was a child; common they might be, but I could not consider leaving them behind.

Our country garden soon billowed with new roses, perennials, trees, larger shrubs and rampant rambling roses. It was wonderful to have the opportunity to grow all those objects of desire that even I could not fit into our first base. The sweet peas were the envy of the neighbours, and we were almost self-sufficient in vegetables for six months of the year. The children were tiny and made no demand on the garden, except for enough lawn for their see-saw rocker, and a place to build a snowman. Fortunately our neighbours had a trampoline and more exciting outdoor toys, so their garden was always more attractive to the youngest end of village society.

The original planting was influenced by what plants I wanted to possess, rather than following any plan of what looked good together and what plant combinations would sustain interest through the year. As in most gardens, it was more often a case of a plant's position being dictated by the space available, rather than the plant being chosen specifically to suit particular growing conditions. As

the garden grew we added and we removed plants, and the more we visited gardens the more we gleaned ideas and adapted them to our own plot. Planting combinations evolved, sometimes by luck, more often by judgement and as a result of inspiration.

We outgrew the house and the garden and embarked upon our Grand Designs era. We moved to a considerably larger house with two acres of land: an undeveloped wilderness. When looking for a plot we wanted one that was south or west facing, in an elevated position, bathed in the evening sun. We opted for a sloping hillside, north-east facing, that lost the sun in the afternoon. I wanted a warm garden with fertile soil; I got a cold garden with impoverished sandy soil. Sometimes life is a compromise. However, I was encouraged when a very talented gardener told me 'To create a garden like mine you need vision, time, energy; and of course, you need to be mad.' I immediately felt that I qualified.

We agreed that we would garden differently now that we had the space. There would be no more little treasures in pots, no more fiddling around with detail. Big bold planting would be the order of the day, with our eye on the bigger picture. Making the transition was not easy, and a large collection of diminutive plants soon built up awaiting a planting position. The first bed around the terrace was quickly colonized by plants brought from our previous garden, including – you've guessed it – forget-me-nots, *Viola cornuta* and wild violets. As so often happens in a garden of any size, I found it difficult to move into the space with the planting. With every decision I gravitated

towards the edges, so the garden retained a bleak and empty look – until we took the brave step to venture into the central void with some bold beds and trees. Immediately the garden started to take shape and become ours.

At any stage of your gardening life this is the moment to work towards, when the garden becomes yours, however large or small the space, whether starting from scratch or developing an existing garden. I know that my present garden will not be mine forever. Eventually it will be time to downsize and move to a smaller plot, hopefully a level one. I intend to approach losing my plot positively, as a new challenge, and as an opportunity to create another new garden of my own, this time taking with me only what I have learned along the way.

*Andrew McIndoe.*

**Top**: Our big plot started to take shape as soon as we broke away from the edges and created beds in the open space. **Centre**: *Myosotis*, forget-me-nots, a childhood favourite. **Above**: The charming lilac-blue flowers of *Viola cornuta*.

# Introduction

At a certain time in your gardening life you have to re-assess the scale of the operation. Whatever the size of your garden, it may be that you can no longer manage it as you have in the past. Too many beds and borders to cultivate, too much grass to cut, too much hard work involved in growing vegetables and pruning fruit trees can mean that you no longer enjoy it as you used to. Here comes the challenge: do you stay put and modify your garden for lower maintenance, or do you downsize and find somewhere more manageable? Either way, with the right approach losing the plot can be a very positive experience.

A large garden may be lovely to look at but it takes a lot of hard work to keep it like this. Just imagine the scale of the task when those leaves fall in autumn.

# Moving on

A big garden may be beautiful but think of all that grass you have to cut, all those leaves you have to collect in autumn, all that pruning and weeding you have to do just to keep your plot in shape.

When it comes to planning your gardening future perhaps the hardest decision is whether you stay where you are and adapt your existing plot to reduce the amount of work involved, or whether you downsize and take on a new garden. The prospect may seem daunting, but do not be put off. Once you look at the various options, you will discover that exciting new possibilities lie ahead, whichever route you decide to take.

## Staying put

If you decide to stay on in your existing home and garden, then you need to take a positive step towards a new approach. You need to identify the aspects of the garden that make it hard work, and decide how to overcome them. This may well mean getting in help, but this will only be successful if you have decided how you are going to manage the garden in the first place. Grassing over the beds, thereby creating even more lawn to mow, may not be the best solution. Also, any changes like this need to be done well, otherwise the result will be disappointing.

People manage plants and gardens in different ways. If you have always taken great care in pruning your shrubs, seeing them trimmed into neat round balls with a hedge-trimmer will be a distressing experience. Take time to find the right person to help you in your garden, someone you can work with to achieve the effect you are looking for.

Be brave and make those decisions that will enable you to keep your garden as something you are proud of, rather than as a burden you have to carry. There are plants you will need to get rid of; there are aspects of gardening that you will no longer be engaged in. Look for new challenges, new content, for your garden, however little. This will help to maintain your interest and love of gardening, while you adjust to the business of change and modification.

## Making the move

It may be that you decide that the best thing is to leave your old garden behind and move on. You may well be losing one plot, but you will have a new one to focus your attention upon – and this may be an empty, brand new garden, or an established one, inherited from someone else. It is always easier to see the potential

for change in something you are not familiar with, and this is certainly true in a garden.

Just as moving from a small garden to a larger one requires a new approach, so losing the plot and downsizing also presents a challenge. The tendency is to try to hang on to what you have: to dig up any plants you can, pot them up and take them with you, regardless of whether or not they are suitable for the new garden. All too frequently some of them then sit in their large transit containers, cluttering up the new patio for several years, slowly sinking into a state of decline.

Those roses might be beautiful, and yes they might move, but is it worth the effort? Since you planted them, new varieties have appeared that produce more flowers, are prone to fewer diseases and have a tidier growth habit. A new rose bush costs a few pounds and you can enjoy choosing it. You might be particularly fond of your spiraea – it was a present from a friend. It is now a woody old plant that, if cut back hard and lifted in the winter, would move to your new garden. There it will look like the woody old shrub it is, and will take a couple of years to regain its former 'glory'. This is hardly the best start for any new garden, of any shape or form, whatever your stage of gardening life. A new shrub such as a spiraea costs about the same as a cheap bottle of wine – so go on, live dangerously and buy a new one.

## A fresh start

The secret is to see any new garden as an opportunity, a fresh start. Downsizing is a positive experience. Yes, you once had a beautiful big garden, which enabled you to grow all sorts of wonderful plants. Perhaps it gave you years of pleasure and was much admired by friends and neighbours. But remember too the other aspect: the hard work, the grass cutting, the ties of watering during summer, leaf sweeping in autumn and clearing up in winter.

Your new, smaller plot offers the opportunity for greater freedom and a higher standard of horticulture and design with less physical effort. Whether you are starting with a blank canvas, or adapting someone else's garden to suit your own taste and needs, you can put more consideration into the planning and the plant selection and more care into the detail of the garden. You can plan it for low maintenance so that it requires little input for the next few years. Alternatively, you can plan a flexible scheme that allows frequent change, and enables you to work in it every day if you wish.

Never say 'I've only got a small garden' in that defeatist way that means 'I've given up and I'm not interested'. If that were true, you would not be reading this book. Remember to announce proudly 'I have a wonderful small garden' in that commanding manner that says 'I only allow the best plants to grow there, every one is hand picked and, if you are coming to look at it, make sure you appreciate what a gem you are looking at!'

**Top:** It's nice to have fruit trees, but can you use all those apples? **Above:** *Rosa* 'Paul's Himalayan Musk' – a beautiful, but decidedly rampant, rambler. **Below:** Time to move on …

# Getting the garden you want

**Above:** Somewhere to sit in the sun and enjoy the garden – without having to walk too far from the house. **Below:** The broad, flat arm of a bench is the perfect place for your mug of tea.

Moving to a brand new plot presents you with a golden opportunity: to shape a garden that is tailored to your needs and to your own particular taste. The process of altering an existing garden to make it more manageable has the same potential: the chance to rethink, to make changes that improve the way the garden works in terms of both looks and practicality. Here are a few thoughts to help you achieve a garden that works for you.

Sometimes it is much easier to see what the garden looks like from photographs. Take a few shots from each viewpoint – the windows of the house, the patio, where you will sit, and the entrance to the garden – and you will get a much clearer idea of what it is really like.

You can also get an impression of what impact various alterations might have, such as adding a tree, widening a border or moving a shed.

## The most important view

When planning the layout of a new garden or evaluating an existing one, it is important to take into account the views from the windows of the house. Most of us spend more time looking at the garden from here than from anywhere else: when we open the curtains in the morning, when we stand at the kitchen sink or sit in the lounge or dining room. Out in the garden we often have a different agenda: weeding, dead-heading, cutting the grass. Certainly we look at the garden and admire it, but more often than not our attention is on specific plants and details rather than on the overall view.

## Make those borders big enough

Give anyone half a dozen shrubs and a garden shed and ask them to create a garden, and nine times out of ten the result will be the same. The shed will go to the far end of the garden, right opposite the windows of the house – perhaps not the most attractive or appropriate focal point. The shrubs will be planted in a narrow border around the edge of the plot – a bed that is barely wide enough to accommodate them now, let alone in two years' time. This immediately creates a maintenance issue, as you will spend future years chopping back the plants, trying to confine them to the space. This usually means that the plants get the blame for growing too large. In reality it is your fault for making the bed far too small.

## Maintain an element of surprise

A good garden does not reveal all of its secrets at the first glance; it invites exploration and discovery and it retains an element of surprise. This will never be achieved by creating narrow borders around three sides of a square plot, which will then be viewed from windows on the remaining side. Fill the middle of the space with grass and all is visible at a glance. By adding a terrace with pots and planting between the terrace and the open space, the picture immediately becomes more interesting. With our desire to populate the boundary of the garden we often overlook this foreground planting. It can have more impact than anything else you do in the garden.

**Above**: A well-planned garden is a picture that only gradually opens to view, rather than being visible all at once. **Left**: A natural wood sculpture adds an element of surprise. **Below**: A pot of tulips provides foreground interest.

Well-filled borders keep weeds at bay. Here a Himalayan birch adds light height, while the tall 'see-through' *Knautia macedonica* in the foreground gives a sense of perspective – altogether a pleasing planting picture, but planned with practicality in mind.

Wherever you are storing tools and equipment, whether in a shed or in the garage, make sure that it is easy to get your wheelbarrow and lawnmower out into the garden. Make the shape of your lawn, if you have one, easy to mow and edge. Also, remember that all gardens, however small, generate waste: you need to be able to compost it or dispose of it without detracting from the garden itself.

If you pay someone to help in the garden, there is another very good reason for ensuring good accessibility and simplicity of maintenance. The quicker and easier it is to do a routine job like grass cutting, the less it costs. Sometimes a few modifications to an existing garden are all that are needed to make it affordable to have someone to do regular maintenance – leaving you free to do the enjoyable gardening.

## Low maintenance or lack of interest?

A low-maintenance design in terms of both structure and planting may be the order of the day, but this should not be at the expense of interest and variety.

Reducing the amount of planting by grassing over the flower beds will not necessarily give you less work: you still have the grass to cut. Leaving space between plants to allow regular forking over and hoeing is not a low-maintenance option either. Adding more hard surfaces may mean there is less gardening to do, but if it makes the garden bleak and uninteresting it is certainly not the right solution. If your beds and borders are full of the right selection of plants, and you have solved any weed problems before planting, then the amount of regular maintenance should be minimal.

## Plan for practicality

However you plan or adapt your garden, always consider the practicality of what you are doing. If you have a patio, make sure it is large enough, and the right shape, to take your table and chairs. Designers frequently advise positioning a sitting area where it will catch the sun at a particular time of day or have the best view. Certainly both these factors are important considerations; however, accessibility is even more important. If you feel like having a cup of coffee outside, you do not always want to carry it the length of the garden before you can sit down and enjoy it.

## Beware of hedges

Hedges and screens are notorious thieves of space and creators of labour. The desire for privacy accounts for more garden disasters than anything else. If the garden is at all open or overlooked, there is an understandable urge to enclose it and shut out the neighbours. If you do this by planting a hedge, you immediately reduce the size of your garden by the space occupied by the hedge, and you rob the adjacent ground of water and nutrients, and potentially light. Worst of all, you give yourself an additional maintenance problem. No hedge grows to a certain height and then stops; hedge cutting is a regular and frequent requirement and demands time and energy, or investment if you use a contractor.

A decorative wooden fence or trellis clothed in well-chosen climbers offers a more immediate solution, takes up less room and requires far less maintenance. Always consider the alternatives.

## Do not become a control freak

The wise gardener understands that plants have never read the rule book and will behave as they will. He or she also allows a plant to have its head and express itself without excessive control. Trimmed, tidy shrubs carefully clipped into spherical shapes ruin many a garden, particularly when they are shrubs that should be allowed to flower or those with a potentially light and airy habit. Topiary is an art of formality, and is wonderful used where originally intended, but not as an unnecessary means of control. Who cares if two neighbouring plants have just proved that you planted them too close together in the first place? Selective removal

of a branch or two from each will give them breathing space, so that they can coexist. This is an occasional operation – whereas regular trimming is drudgery.

A fear of heights is not uncommon among gardeners. As soon as a shrub dares to stick its head above the fence it is cut back. Just as a tree starts to reach its potential it is beheaded. Think carefully before you take action. Just because a plant gets a bit bigger than you had imagined, does it matter? Removing the top of a woody plant usually stimulates vigorous growth further down, which exacerbates the problem. If possible, use selective thinning of the branches to allow light and rain to pass through to plants beneath, rather than reducing the height. It is the natural height provided by tall shrubs and trees that transforms a garden from being flat and uninteresting to becoming a three-dimensional space.

**Above left**: Both *Daphne bholua* 'Jacqueline Postill' and *Berberis thunbergii* 'Starburst' (**above**) have an attractive natural habit that would be ruined by control-freak pruning. **Below**: Low in maintenance but high in interest: *Phormium* 'Sundowner' adds contrasting form and colour to geraniums and alliums.

# The way ahead

Having made the decision to move to a smaller garden or to stay put and adapt your existing plot, you now face another challenge: how to create the garden you want for this stage in your life. This may involve some radical changes: altering the hard surfaces, reducing or getting rid of the lawn, modifying beds and borders, removing existing shrubs and replanting. Now is the time to make these major decisions, rather than living with things that spoil the effect and stand in the way of what you are trying to achieve. Do not let thoughts of the enormity of the task overpower your decision to create a new garden, one that will provide what you are looking for – something lovely to look at, a place to sit, and a place to indulge in your passion for plants.

Permanently planted containers, grouped together with pots of bulbs, create a colourful picture on this terrace. A scheme of this type would work in the smallest garden.

# Keeping a lawn

An immaculate, well-tended lawn certainly sets off the garden beautifully. If you want stripes, you need a good mower and a level site.

Most gardens feature a lawn of some description, and to many gardeners a garden does not look right without one. Some take pride in their lawn and get pleasure from keeping it immaculately trimmed and tended. To others, maintaining the lawn is a task that has to be endured, and mowing it is just part of a weekly routine that gets in the way of life's more pleasurable activities. In both cases, it is worth considering ways of making lawn maintenance easier, and these apply whether you have a small garden or a larger plot, and whether you are making a new lawn or dealing with an existing one.

## Mowers and mowing

The condition of the lawn has a profound effect on any garden. In a small space a lawn has to be maintained to the highest standards, otherwise it will simply detract from the rest of the garden. Regular mowing is essential, and for this to be a pleasure rather than a chore you need the right mower for the job. The cheapest available machine from your local DIY store is rarely the best choice, and you should never assume that because you have a small lawn you only need a cheap, light mower.

Today most mowers are rotary mowers, in other words they cut with a rotating blade. These can give just as fine a cut as a classic cylinder mower. Mulch mowers are increasingly popular. These chop up the grass cuttings and blow them down between the grass plants onto the soil surface. Here they decompose and act as mulch, as well as improving the soil. They are successful only if the grass is cut regularly and kept at a height of 2–3cm (¾–1in).

Scalping the lawn in summer, in the belief that you will then not need to cut it so often, is the road to ruin for your lawn. It puts the grass plants under pressure, allowing weeds and moss to populate the turf and, if there is a period of drought, it will quickly result in brown grass.

## Shape and size

All too often, the inclination is to stick with a lawn's existing shape, whether or not it is pleasing to the eye, or easy to mow and maintain. Many gardens can be improved simply by modifying the shape of the lawn, even if only to soften edges and do away with awkward corners that are hard to mow.

Consult a garden machinery specialist and choose a machine that handles well and suits the size of your lawn. You need one with a grass box that is easy to empty, if you intend to collect the cuttings (you may want to use the machine for leaf collection in the autumn anyway). Most of all, you need one that will cut the lawn and leave it with the best possible finish.

**Right**: A well-installed gravel mowing strip separates the planting from the grass and makes mowing easier. **Below right**: A path across a lawn *must* be at the right level if you want neat, easy-to-maintain edges.

Lawns do not have to be square; they can be round, oval or kidney shaped. Simple shapes work best, however, and wiggly edges should be avoided at all costs. Soft, sweeping curves are most attractive and, as most plots are square, oblong or triangular, a rounded lawn is usually the most successful: this naturally creates planting areas of varying widths and encourages deeper planting into the corners.

## Manoeuvring and edging

If lawn maintenance is going to be trouble-free, the shape of the lawn must make it easy to manoeuvre the mower without having to step on the flower beds or change direction unnecessarily. We soon get used to tricky areas of our gardens and learn to live with them. However, adjusting the shape of the lawn and planting areas to make it easier and less laborious to cut the grass will save a surprising amount of time and effort.

The same is true when it comes to the edges of the lawn. If you install a good-quality metal or heavy plastic edging to support the edges of the lawn, you may be able to mow over it to trim the edges without needing to use shears. Alternatively, a mowing strip of brick or stone paviors around the edge of the lawn separates the grass from the flower beds and does away with the need to edge the lawn to keep it in shape. This sounds ideal in theory, but it must be done extremely well to be successful. The stones or bricks for the mowing strip must be set very slightly below the ground surface to avoid damaging the mower.

It is this difficulty in getting the levels just right that causes problems where areas of paving,

such as the patio, meet the lawn. Usually the paving stands slightly above the grass, making maintenance tricky. The result is an untidy edge that never looks right. This can be overcome by adding an area of planting between patio and lawn, or at least laying a narrow strip of stone chippings between them, sitting about 1cm (½in) below the ground surface. This sharpens the edge of the lawn, so it looks neater, and makes it easier to maintain.

# Living without a lawn

Never opt for cheap, poor-quality slabs. There is a tendency to think that just because you are choosing a surface for the garden, rather than a carpet for the sitting room, the decision is less important. It is not. The paving will have a strong impact on the appearance of the garden and you want to lay it only once. Choose paving that looks good with the brick of the house and the style of the garden. Using paviors of different sizes usually looks more interesting than slabs all of the same size, and soft, subtle colours enhance the planting rather than fighting with it.

Paving is a good choice in open, sunny situations but you should beware of using it in shaded areas overhung by trees. Algae can make paved surfaces very slippery and hazardous during damp winter weather.

**Above**: A carpet of thymes and other low mound- and mat-forming shrubs is punctuated with pots of colourful bedding plants. **Right**: Feathery santolina softens a rather rough area of paving.

Unless you are a dab hand at hard landscaping it is always better to have paving professionally installed by an experienced contractor. Think twice before asking your local handyman or part-time gardener to do it – you may be disappointed with the result, and it is not easy to alter badly laid paving.

In a small garden you may decide to do away with the lawn altogether. A very small area of grass can be difficult to mow, and it means that you have to have somewhere to store a mower. But in place of grass you could use paving, gravel, water, or low ground-hugging plants. All of these will fulfil the same role as grass in creating an open space between the areas of planting.

## Paving

Paving is a possible alternative to grass in a small area; it provides a hard surface that can be used in all weathers and a firm, level base for pots and containers. There is a great variety of different types of natural stone and concrete slabs available, and it is important to choose wisely, to make sure you get it right first time.

## Gravel – the soft option

Gravel is a soft surface that is simple to install, and blends easily into planted areas. Some may be wary of it, imagining it to be an untidy

An easy-to-maintain gravel pathway winds through an area of undulating planting, softening the overall effect and inviting leisurely exploration.

Think about blending and mixing different shades and sizes of stones – the variety of colours and textures is infinite. You can also use different types of stones in some areas to create particular effects, for example to resemble a dry stream bed; when combined with the right planting this can be very successful.

surface that scatters and invites visits from neighbourhood cats. While this can be true of traditional pea shingle, there are many different types of stone chippings and larger pebbles that give a much more stable result.

On flat sites you can use a fabric membrane under the stone to give permanent weed control. You must use a top-quality landscape fabric for this, and anchor it well with fixing pins onto firm, level ground, before laying the stone chippings to a depth of at least 6cm (2½in). Bury the edges vertically into the ground otherwise they will eventually work their way up through the gravel, spoiling the effect. Bear in mind that small stone chippings will tend to move around on the surface, and never use a membrane under stones on a sloping site because the chippings will quickly slip to the bottom of the slope.

A more stable solution, and certainly the best method on an uneven or sloping site, is to use a composite aggregate base such as scalpings or hoggin, which consists of stone pieces bound together with clay. This is spread over the surface of firmed ground and rolled with a heavy roller to compact it. The gravel or stone chippings are then laid on top to a depth of 4cm (1½in) or more, and these will bind into the aggregate base to give a firmer surface. You may get some weeds appearing through the gravel, but these are easily controlled with a path weedkiller. This method also allows you to encourage plants and bulbs to grow through the gravel in selected areas.

The simplest way to lay a loose stone surface is directly onto compacted ground. As long as the site is weed-free there is no reason not to do this. The gravel or chippings must be at least 6cm (2½in) deep. Although you will undoubtedly get some weeds growing after a period of time, you will be able to plant directly into the gravel to give a softer effect, and some of your plants will seed themselves among the stones, which will look pleasingly naturalistic.

# Planting in gravel

Where gravel is used as an alternative to a lawn, creeping, carpeting plants can be introduced to create a greener, softer effect. Many of these change colour and texture during the course of the year, either when they produce flowers or when the foliage tints in autumn and winter.

1

2

**Creeping thymes** are lovely plants for creating a 'lawn' in gravel. Their stems hug the ground, their aromatic foliage releases its fragrance when walked upon, and the colourful fragrant flowers, which appear in early summer, are loved by butterflies, bees and other pollinating insects. They do especially well in hot, sunny situations. There are many varieties of *Thymus serpyllum* to choose from, with white, pink, purple or red flowers. ***Thymus serpyllum 'Minimalist'*** (1) is one of the smallest, most compact varieties, with tiny leaves and mauve flowers. ***Thymus serpyllum 'Pink Chintz'*** (2) is a favourite, with profuse soft pink flowers. *Thymus* Coccineus Group is especially striking, with bright crimson–purple flowers. ***Thymus 'Doone Valley'*** (3) is a lemon-scented thyme with larger leaves of dark green, irregularly marked with gold, and purple-pink flowers.

Enjoying similar conditions, **creeping sedums** or stonecrops offer an even wider variety of colours and textures, with both their foliage and their early summer flowers. These succulent plants can exist without soil, and are extensively used for green roofs and architectural features. Planted in gravel in the garden, they become living stones and are especially useful on exposed sites and near the coast; in fact, some are found clinging to seaside walls and on rocky cliffs.

***Sedum dasyphyllum*** (4) has tiny grey-green leaves tightly packed on short stems. It thrives in partial shade as well as full sun. *Sedum acre* 'Aureum' has bright green foliage on crowded shoots, with vivid yellow flowers. The varieties of *Sedum album* have tiny shining leaves that resemble large rice grains threaded on thin stems;

3

4

5

6

When planting into gravel scrape away the stones from an area at least 30cm (12in) in diameter. Dig a hole wider and deeper than you need for your new plant, piling the soil onto a piece of polythene or a large tray. Break up the soil in the bottom of the hole and, if it is heavy, add some sharp grit. Replace some of the soil, mixed with planting compost and slow-release fertilizer. Position the plant, then fill around it with soil mixed with planting compost; firm and water thoroughly. Replace the gravel around the plant. If you give the individual plants a good start they will establish quickly and soon reward with a show of new growth.

creeping forms. *Sedum spathulifolium* 'Cape Blanco' is a good grey-leaved form and contrasts well with **Sedum spathulifolium 'Purpureum'** (6), a more vigorous spreading form with wine-red foliage. Both produce starry yellow flowers. All of these varieties are evergreen.

It is also worth including sedums that die back in the winter as they help to change the appearance of the area when they start into growth in spring. The varieties of *Sedum spurium* fall into this category. **Sedum spurium 'Fuldaglut'** (7) has dark red foliage and rosy red flowers.

Some of the dwarf **dianthus** (pinks) are excellent carpeting plants, often with steely grey-green foliage and brilliantly coloured flowers. They are particularly successful on alkaline soils. *Dianthus deltoides* is a mat-forming plant with fine stems carrying tiny bright blooms. *Dianthus deltoides* 'Brilliant' has bright carmine-pink flowers and **Dianthus deltoides 'Leuchtfunk' (Flashing Light)** (8) has cerise blooms. Any of the mound-forming dwarf pinks with tightly packed leaves are

worth including as a mossy contrast to creeping varieties of thyme and sedum; there are many excellent varieties. Select from the alpine range at your local garden centre in late spring or early summer, when they are in bloom.

A number of different types of **phlox** form low mats or cushions smothered with colourful fragrant flowers in late spring and early summer. Their foliage is not at its best later in the season and they look drab in winter, but they are worth considering for their brilliant floral display. The advantage of growing phlox in gravel is that they become virtually invisible when the leaves turn a pale brown as they fade into semi-dormancy. *Phlox douglasii* cultivars form mats 30cm (12in) or so across, as do those of *Phlox subulata*, the moss phlox. **Phlox douglasii 'Rosea'** (9), with mauve-pink

flowers, is a good partner for pink and purple thymes. *Phlox douglasii* 'Boothman's Variety' has lavender-blue flowers that have a deeper blue eye. **Phlox subulata 'Emerald Cushion Blue'** (10) is a compact plant forming a mound of evergreen foliage studded with lilac-blue flowers in spring and early summer.

they have either white or pink flowers. **Sedum album 'Coral Carpet'** (5) is an attractive form with leaves that turn coral red in hot, dry conditions.

*Sedum spathulifolium* has broader, blunt-ended leaves carried in rosettes and forms more of a mound than the

*Acaena microphylla* (11), the New Zealand bur, is a strong-growing carpeting plant with attractive compact fern-like foliage and large spiky seedheads in mid- to late summer. The variety *Acaena microphylla* 'Kupferteppich' (Copper Carpet) is one of the best, with deep coppery foliage and large red burs held just above the ground. This is excellent in any carpet-planting scheme involving gravel or paving because its main season of interest comes after the earlier-blooming thymes and sedums.

Where the soil is more moist, *Pratia pedunculata* (12) is delightful grown in gravel. This forms a mat of tiny bright green leaves studded with starry sky-blue flowers from early summer until mid-autumn. Where it is happy it spreads rapidly and will even naturalize in grass.

*Mentha requienii* (13), Corsican mint, is another moisture-lover for sun or partial shade. Small, fragrant dark green leaves and lilac flowers in summer are carried on low stems that creep in the gaps between stones and pebbles. Like creeping thyme, it is a delight to walk on.

The creeping bugle, *Ajuga reptans*, is a versatile plant used extensively in pots and containers, and as ground cover in semi-shade. It grows successfully in open sunny conditions too, and its shining leaves and spikes of bright flowers in late spring and early summer are a good contrast to the smaller, softer leaves of other carpeting plants. There are pink and white flowering forms but those with sapphire flowers and burgundy foliage are the most striking and useful.

*Ajuga reptans* 'Atropurpurea' is the most widely grown bugle. It spreads by means of creeping stems that throw up perky rosette-shaped plantlets over a wide area. The foliage is purple-brown, but in an open, sunny position it looks a much richer colour. *Ajuga reptans* 'Black Scallop' (14) is a newer variety with larger, rounded purple-black leaves. The growth habit is more compact and less spreading. For a softer effect, grow *Ajuga reptans* 'Burgundy Glow' (15), which has attractive pink, purple and grey-green marbled foliage. It looks good alongside purple-leaved heucheras grown in pots or at the edge of a neighbouring border.

There is a host of other plants that can be added to a gravel lawn to increase variety and turn it into a delightful tapestry of texture and colour. The succulent

In coastal gardens, or to create a seaside look, you can introduce maritime natives such as thrift (*Armeria maritima*) and sea campion (*Silene schafta*). These form low mounds and from late spring into summer provide bright pink and white flowers respectively.

rosettes of sempervivums (houseleeks) will revel on the stony surface in full sun. Spiky dwarf sisyrinchiums, with their charming blue or yellow starry flowers in summer, add a contrasting form, and self-seeding Californian poppies provide vibrant summer colour. Mossy saxifrages and those with white-frosted rosettes will grow well and bloom freely in spring and early summer. In spring, species

crocus, dwarf narcissi and irises, chionodoxa, muscari and scillas add early colour. In autumn and late winter, hardy cyclamen delight with their exquisite flowers and fabulously marbled leaves.

**Top left**: *Armeria maritima*, thrift, makes neat cushions smothered with flowers in spring and summer. **Above left**: *Eschscholzia californica*, Californian poppies, seed themselves freely in gravel. **Above**: *Iris bucharica* 'Foster' and *Muscari botryoides* 'Album' bloom alongside bright blue veronica.

Gravel and stone chippings are wonderful around plants. They keep the wet of the winter off the foliage, and reflect sunlight from the surface of the ground, keeping it cooler, and possibly moister, in summer. Under dwarf evergreen shrubs and conifers the reflected light keeps the underside of the foliage a more even colour. In addition to low carpeting plants, a gravel bed works particularly well with Mediterranean and silver foliage shrubs, dwarf bulbs and alpines; and it looks good with architectural plants such as phormiums and grasses.

# Banishing weeds

One of the most effective ways to make your gardening life easier is to reduce the presence of weeds in your plot. Weeds compete with cultivated plants and will always get the upper hand if left unchecked, stealing every opportunity to colonize available ground. Gardens infested with weeds require constant attention throughout the growing season, and this is boring, frustrating and time-consuming. Fortunately, there are a number of ways to reduce the problem to a minimum.

If you are starting a garden from scratch, overcome any weed infestation before you begin to plant, even if it means delaying most of the planting for a season while you tackle the weeds. You could still go ahead and plant one or two shrubs and trees, and have seasonal planting in containers; but for the time being avoid planting any perennials, ground cover and low-growing shrubs because they will make the use of herbicides virtually impossible.

If you are trying to make an existing garden lower maintenance then you need to take a hard line. Weed-infested beds may mean that you have to sacrifice the ornamental plants to conquer the weeds; no herbicide can tell the difference between a cultivated plant and a weed. This might be heartbreaking, but in the long run it will be worthwhile. A bed of perennials overrun with ground elder will never be your garden's greatest asset, and no matter how many hours you spend painting the leaves of the weeds with herbicide, you will still be defeated.

Weeds such as dandelion (**left**) and hairy bittercress (**below**) seed prolifically. The secret of success in controlling them is to remove them before they seed and spread throughout your garden.

If you have a bed of herbaceous perennials infested with perennial weeds and you want to save some of the plants, try lifting and potting the most treasured ones and tackle the problem using containers. Dig up clumps of the plants, pot them in quality potting compost in large plastic pots, and keep them out of the way in a corner of the garden. When the weeds are in full leaf, spray the whole bed with a systemic herbicide; you may need to do this several times during the growing season. Also treat the leaves of any weeds that appear among the plants in the pots, carefully applying the herbicide with a paintbrush. When you are sure that all weeds in the bed and the pots have been killed, you can replant in the bed; before you do so, cultivate the soil thoroughly and add a general fertilizer and soil conditioner such as garden compost or well-rotted stable manure.

Weed-control membranes always seem like a wonderful idea, particularly to gardeners who already have a perennial weed problem. However, a membrane will not get rid of perennial weeds. The weeds will almost certainly find their way to the surface at the membrane edges and through the planting holes. The ground must be free of perennial weeds before you lay the membrane, and the job must be done well to be successful.

**Right**: Always have a suitable bag or bucket available to collect weeds as you notice them in the border.
**Below**: Growing bindweed up a cane makes it easy to treat with a systemic weedkiller.

## Perennial weeds

Perennial weeds are those with root systems that enable them to survive, usually underground, from season to season. Bindweed, ground elder, nettle, thistle, mare's tail and couch grass are a few examples of pernicious weeds, and these are the curse of many gardens. The target here is the roots: you must get rid of these to get rid of the problem. If you attempt to dig them out, any fragments left behind act as root cuttings, and the weeds regenerate. Your access to the roots is through the leaves with a systemic herbicide (one containing glyphosate is widely used). This type of herbicide is inactivated once it is in contact with the ground, so it must be sprayed on the actively growing foliage of the weeds to be effective (it will of course kill any other plants whose foliage it touches). Obviously the more leaves there are, the more chemical gets into the weeds to kill the roots, so best results are achieved at the height of the growing season.

## Annual weeds

Annual weeds are successful because they complete their growth cycle quickly, growing,

flowering and setting seed in just a few weeks. It is the seeds that are your enemy. The secret of control is to interrupt the life cycle before the weeds set seed, and to prevent germination of any seeds already in the soil. The seeds usually need to be near the surface to germinate, so cultivating the soil can result in a whole new crop. However, these weeds mostly have shallow roots, so hoeing when the weeds are young disturbs the roots and kills them. Mulching with bark or another material that buries the seeds well below the surface is an efficient means of control. Herbicides kill growing annual weeds easily, but often not before seeds have been produced. Whatever method you use, keeping on top of the problem for a season or two is the answer; remember: one year's seeds means seven years' weeds.

## Weed-control membranes

The idea of a weed-control membrane to prevent weeds ever seeing the light of day in your beds and borders is undoubtedly appealing. It is this promise that is responsible for countless rolls of membrane being sold to gardeners every year. The principle is simple: a layer of permeable fabric covers the ground around the border plants; weeds cannot grow through it, but water and air can pass through to the soil beneath. However, you need to bear in mind that a membrane is difficult to lay around existing planting, and is best used on new beds and borders, before the plants are put in place (see also box on page 25). Topping with a loose mulch such as bark will disguise its rather utilitarian appearance. It can also be used under paving and gravel (see page 19).

Alchemilla, eryngium, achillea, phormium and a variety of other perennials form a dense cover in the border, leaving little if any room for emerging weeds.

The surface of the ground must be level before the membrane is laid. You can use it on a slope, before ground cover is planted for example, but you cannot cover it with mulch. If you do, the mulch will simply slide down to the bottom. Where a border runs alongside a path, patio or lawn, the soil level needs to be lower than the adjoining surface, otherwise any mulch used over the membrane will migrate onto the lawn or path.

There are various grades of membrane available; always buy the best quality, as you want it to last as long as possible. You can usually choose either black or brown. If you intend to use it on a slope, where it will be exposed until ground-cover plants become established, opting for brown will mean the area looks less like a motorway embankment.

You must anchor the fabric firmly with pegs or pins, available from membrane suppliers. Position the plants and cut a cross in the fabric beneath each one. Open up the fabric at these points, plant and then re-lay the fabric up to the plant stems. Be sure to bury the edges: bits of membrane sticking up around the plants are not attractive. Now cover with whichever loose mulch you have decided to use.

This method can be highly successful around trees and shrubs, but it does not work with most

perennials, and it does not allow you to add bulbs and annuals to the planting. If topping with bark mulch, make sure it is of good quality, consisting of large chips or nuggets; lightweight mulches soon move, exposing the fabric, particularly if laid too thinly.

## Loose mulches

A loose mulch is essentially a layer of material placed over the soil surface around plants to suppress weeds by depriving them of the light they need for growth. It will also help retain moisture, and can be effective at keeping the ground cool in summer and warm in winter. Organic materials such as bark, compost and straw are most often used; gravel and pebbles are also suitable in some settings.

## Bark mulch

The material most commonly used as weed-suppressing mulch is chipped pine bark, a by-product of the timber industry. It is

**Above**: A generous mulch of bark chips keeps weeds at bay and helps to conserve moisture. It looks good too. **Below left**: Perennials such as hostas love a mulch of composted chipped wood waste.

Installing enough bark mulch to be effective is not inexpensive. If you are doubtful about whether it will be successful, do just one area and evaluate how much maintenance it saves in a season, with a view to doing the other planting areas the following year, if it works for you. Most gardeners soon decide to do the rest of the garden.

**Above:** Covering the compost in pots with a layer of grit or stone chippings helps to prevent it drying out. **Below right:** Slate scree works well as a mulch and is decorative. It can be used to create the effect of a dry stream bed.

A number of recycled materials are marketed as weed-suppressing, moisture-retaining garden mulches. Chipped rubber, made from old tyres, is just one of these. This is not an organic substance, it does not decompose with time, and once you have spread it on your borders it will be impossible to get rid of. Think carefully before you use any unknown material in your garden.

unobtrusive in the garden, and if laid properly can be effective at reducing maintenance and conserving soil moisture. The main reason for failure or disappointing results is that the bark is spread too thinly. It needs to be in a layer at least 6cm (2½in) deep if it is to work, and must be topped up every two to three years. Any organic matter such as bark gradually decomposes and in doing so can take nitrogen from the soil, depriving plants growing there. The harder, better-quality bark chips and nuggets decompose more slowly and so the amount of nitrogen they take is negligible.

Bark mulch can be laid directly on the soil surface or over a fabric membrane (see pages 26–27). Before laying it directly onto soil, make sure the ground is weed-free; the soil must also be moist, so autumn and early spring are the best times to apply it.

Bark works well around trees, shrubs and more vigorous perennials, and bulbs will be able to push through it. It is not ideal where you intend to grow annuals. If your beds are mounded above adjoining paths and lawns, the mulch will spill onto the surrounding surfaces, aided by pets and birds; this is inevitable. In this case it may be better to lay a deep mulch in the middle of the bed, leaving the edges to be covered by ground-cover planting.

## Other types of loose mulch

The composted green waste from council recycling schemes, readily available in most areas, can be used as a loose mulch for beds and borders. Just like the material from your own compost heap, it should have been composted at a temperature high enough to kill weed seeds. In reality this does not always happen, and by using it you may be introducing a new weed problem. Ideally you should apply it in autumn; any weeds will start to appear early the following spring and you will have time to take action before everything really gets going later in the season. (Compost also makes an excellent soil conditioner, and for this purpose can be dug into the ground at any time of year.)

Mulch made from mineralized straw is light to handle and attractive. It is an excellent choice for the vegetable garden, where it can be dug in at the end of the season as a soil conditioner. Straw breaks down easily in the soil, but mineralization slows this process, making the straw suitable for use as mulch. Because it is light and fine it is also a good choice around perennials, such as hostas, which will appreciate its water-conservation properties.

Wood chips, usually made from wood waste, are useful in certain areas. If you have a tree removed from the garden, you can ask the contractor to chip the branches and anything else that has not been logged, and use this material as mulch. It is better to leave the chips to stand for a few months to start the composting process before applying them. If laid immediately, they will take nitrogen from the soil and slow the growth of plants; this can actually be beneficial if used alongside mature hedges and evergreen shrubs. There are various bagged woodchip products available, including artificially coloured 'decorative' mulches. These might seem like a good idea but they should be avoided; in the natural environment of a garden they look ghastly.

In dry gardens, for Mediterranean effect and near the coast, gravel, pebbles or crushed seashells are a good choice for mulch. Seashell mulch is popular in parts of Europe and is a by-product of the seafood industry. It is relatively light to use, attractive and bright in appearance.

Gravel and pieces of stone laid over the soil surface show off the plants growing there and make it simple to remove any weeds, if they appear.

## Mulch from your garden

If your garden generates a sufficient amount of waste it is worth considering a shredder, which will chew up branches and prunings and spit them out as chippings. These can be used as a mulch, ideally after they have matured for two or three months. You need somewhere to store this piece of equipment and somewhere to use it, and you need a good-quality machine that is quiet in operation, otherwise you will find the shredding process unpleasant.

You can use grass cuttings as a weed-suppressing mulch around mature trees and shrubs. This can look unsightly as the grass decomposes, but is perhaps more tolerable at the back of a border – and is a good way of getting rid of the clippings. Positioning a few paving stones through the planting would make access easy for you to do this.

Of course, you can also use your own home-made garden compost as mulch. This is excellent, as long as you can be sure it is not full of weed seeds. Composted leaves from deciduous trees make a good weed-suppressing mulch, if you compost them with a few grass cuttings and use them before they have completely broken down into leaf mould.

# Planting for low maintenance

Small-leaved hebes and trimmed box create a pleasing low-maintenance planting. Given the right spacing, they cover the ground efficiently, suppressing any annual weeds.

Professional designers and gardeners recommend planting perennials and smaller shrubs, such as lavender and santolina, in threes or fives or more, rather than singly, because a larger group will have more impact. But this all depends on the space you have. You must judge for yourself whether the use of bigger groups of single varieties will be in proportion to the size of the garden and will achieve the effect you are looking for.

When you are trying to reduce the level of maintenance your garden requires, or planning a new garden that you don't want to be too demanding of your time, it is important to take a good look at the plants you grow to make sure they work for you rather than the other way round. How they grow, and how quickly, will dictate the amount of attention you need to give them. The number of different plants you include, and whether they are in the ground or in containers, will also affect the time you will need to spend.

## Find the correct spacing

Spacing plants correctly is one of the hardest things to get right in any garden. If you are aiming for low maintenance, bear in mind that planting too far apart results in gaps – in other words, spaces for weeds to invade. If you plant too close together, then some subjects will be overwhelmed by the competition, and you will need to devote time and energy to restoring discipline. It is always hard to believe that anything in a one-litre pot can potentially occupy one square metre of ground. Knowing how long it will take to do this, and what you can do in the meantime to fill the gaps, comes with experience. If you need advice, consult a good reference book or seek help from staff at the garden centre or nursery.

## Choose the right plants

As a general rule, shrubs are lower maintenance than herbaceous perennials. Shrubs retain their structure and size during the winter months, even if they shed their leaves. Most herbaceous perennials die down to ground level over winter, so they require a certain amount of cleaning up of faded stems and foliage, and many need some sort of support to stop them falling over. There are exceptions. Roses are shrubs that need regular pruning, dead-heading and feeding as well as spraying to keep them in good condition. Bergenias and heucheras are herbaceous, but both are evergreen and need little maintenance, apart from the removal of a few dead leaves and the odd old flower stem.

The nearest you can get to a low-maintenance garden plant is a small shrub that grows relatively slowly, and has a consistent mature size. These are the tried and tested garden favourites: *Hebe* 'Red Edge', *Euonymus fortunei* 'Emerald 'n' Gold', *Spiraea japonica* 'Firelight', *Sarcococca confusa*, to name but a few. Do not spurn them just because they are common; use them as the foundation of a planting scheme and you will find you are well on the way to a low-maintenance result.

Dwarf and slow-growing conifers are low-maintenance plants. They do not need to be pruned, and they retain their foliage and appearance throughout the year. Once established, they are drought-resistant and tolerant, with a predictable growth rate and ultimate size.

As we have seen, not all perennials are hard work. The secret of success is to do your research before you buy them. For example, some, such as peonies, astilbes, hostas and daylilies, can go for years without needing to be lifted, divided and replanted; on the other hand, the performance of bearded irises declines after three or four years if they are not divided and rejuvenated. Herbaceous geraniums, such as the long-flowering *Geranium* 'Jolly Bee' or *Geranium* 'Rozzanne', and that old favourite *Alchemilla mollis* need little attention, provide good ground cover and one way or another contribute to the planting picture for much of the year. These are just the kind of plants you should be looking for in a low-maintenance scheme.

## Limit your plant palette

As long as you choose reliable plants of limited ultimate size, you can reduce maintenance further by restricting the palette of plants you use. If most of your plants require the same growing conditions, and the same annual cycle of maintenance, then your gardening regime will be simpler than if you grow more varied and challenging subjects. Now, in reality most gardeners will always want a few challenges, so the aim must be to reach a compromise between low maintenance, retaining interest and having enough gardening to do.

The other advantage of limiting your plant palette is that it simplifies the design of the garden. By using the same plant in several locations you increase its impact, and produce a more unified effect. This will also help to create a more balanced picture in terms of colour, texture and form. Simplicity is always striking, and a small space can look very effective when planted with only two or three well-chosen varieties.

## Restrict seasonal planting to containers

Annuals are a great way of adding colour and they are undoubtedly useful to fill gaps in a bed or border while the permanent planting fills out. In the long term, however, seasonal bedding plants in the ground are high maintenance, because they need replacing twice a year. If you limit their use to containers they are easier to manage, and the main planting scheme of the garden remains independent of them.

**Above**: *Picea pungens* 'Globosa' is a striking, slow-growing conifer that remains attractive throughout the year. **Below**: A romantic combination of achilleas, geraniums and perovskia looks good through summer into early autumn.

# Going for ground cover

A ground-cover plant should do exactly what the name suggests: cover the ground. In doing so, it should also suppress weeds and maintain interest. For a ground-cover subject to be successful in achieving low maintenance it needs to be vigorous enough to work, but well-behaved enough not to take over.

In a smaller garden some ground-cover plants are just too invasive. *Rubus tricolor*, for example, is marvellous for ground cover on a steep

bank, or a big space under large shrubs and trees, but use it in a small garden and it will soon smother everything else, including the house. *Cotoneaster dammeri*, on the other hand, is still vigorous but stays close to the ground, forming a mat of small glossy green leaves studded with white flowers in spring, followed by red berries.

The plants described on these pages are all good for providing ground cover in smaller gardens. Most are especially useful in shady spots. For ideas for ground cover in sun see *Planting in gravel*, pages 20–23.

## 1 *Ajuga reptans* 'Atropurpurea'

This purple-leaved bugle spreads by horizontal stems, producing evergreen rosettes of crinkled, shining, wine-coloured leaves along the way. Short spikes of sapphire flowers arise in spring. It is excellent for ground cover in semi-shade, as long as conditions are not too dry.

## 2 *Asarum europaeum*

A choice evergreen for ground cover in shade, asarum has rounded, slightly cupped, glossy green leaves carried on short stems. It is compact and spreads slowly, so is valuable where a non-invasive plant is required. Once established it is effective and attractive.

## 3 *Brunnera macrophylla*

With heart-shaped, velvety green leaves and bright blue spring flowers resembling forget-me-nots, brunnera has a lot going for it as a garden plant. It is not a ground-hugger, but soon spreads in semi-shade and will colonize the ground under larger shrubs and areas planted with spring-flowering bulbs. There

are variegated forms (see page 126) but the species is the best for general ground cover.

## 4 *Epimedium* × *rubrum*

This is an evergreen epimedium with heart-shaped leaves on dainty stems. The new leaves are tinted red and the foliage often colours well in winter. Once established, it is one of the best ground-cover plants for partial shade. Epimediums often look thin and weak in their containers at the nursery or garden centre; do not let this put you off planting them.

## 5 *Galium odoratum*

Sweet woodruff is a woodland perennial with whorls of narrow bright green leaves on fine short stems topped with tiny sparkling white flowers in spring. Although it dies down in winter, its dense network of underground stems and the early emergence of its foliage make it effective as a ground-cover plant. You can tidy up by removing the faded foliage in winter, or you can leave it on the soil surface – the plant will soon grow through it the following spring.

**5**

## 6 Geranium macrorrhizum

This is a low-growing geranium with aromatic, mainly evergreen foliage that colours well in autumn and winter. Bright pink flowers on short stems emerge in late spring. The plant spreads by horizontal rhizomes on the soil surface. These form a dense network and, with the leaves, create useful ground cover in sun or shade. It is a good choice around the base of deciduous trees.

## 7 Hedera helix 'Glacier'

Many varieties of small-leaved ivy provide excellent evergreen ground cover. Some gardeners have a fear of ivy, imagining that it will smother everything in its path, but many varieties are reasonably well behaved – you just need to exercise a little control. The ever-popular *Hedera helix* 'Glacier' has leaves marbled with a pleasing grey-green.

Shade-tolerant ground-cover plants come into their own beneath larger perennials and shrubs. As well as suppressing weeds, they fill the gaps in the early stages of a planting scheme, so it looks a little less sparse. If you choose evergreens you will have interest in winter when deciduous subjects lose their leaves. *Vinca minor* f. *alba*, for example, would work well beneath *Cornus mas* 'Variegata'. The vinca's foliage remains a rich dark green when the cornus loses its leaves, and it sets off the shrub's early yellow flowers. In spring, the vinca's white flowers add further interest, especially when the white and green leaves of the cornus unfurl.

## 8 Lamium maculatum 'White Nancy'

This is a lovely subject for shade, its silver-marked leaves forming a shining mat on creeping stems, with pretty white flowers in summer. For a little more colour, try 'Beacon Silver', which has purple-pink flowers. Both will withstand dry conditions, so are useful at the base of a wall or under trees.

## 9 Tiarella cordifolia

This is an unassuming but hard-working plant with light green heart-shaped leaves and delicate spikes of sparkling white flowers in

**6**

**7**

**8**

summer. It is a good choice for ground cover in shade, especially under white-variegated evergreens such as *Euonymus japonicus* 'Kathy'.

## 10 Vinca minor 'Illumination'

There are many varieties of the lesser periwinkle that make excellent ground-cover plants. These are not as invasive or vigorous as *Vinca major*, especially if you choose those with variegated leaves. *Vinca minor* 'Illumination' has creeping stems carrying golden yellow leaves, edged with dark green. It forms an evergreen mat of bright foliage studded with

sapphire flowers in spring. It is cheerful and striking, and a perfect partner for early yellow narcissi such as *Narcissus* 'February Gold'.

**9**

**10**

# Making the garden accessible

**Left**: Well-built raised beds show off plants and make maintenance easy. The wide pathway allows easy access whatever the weather.

If you are to maintain and enjoy your garden you need to plan for accessibility, according to your ability and agility. Steps may look great, but if they are impossible to negotiate with a wheelbarrow or the mower, you need to think again. If you find bending is becoming a problem, it may be worth considering bringing part of the garden up to a more comfortable level with raised beds or planters.

It is always surprising what we learn to live with. When we move into a new home a feature that initially seems rather awkward, or illogical, soon becomes something that we accept or simply cease to notice − that is, if it is not changed within the first few weeks. The same is true of gardens.

If you are modifying an existing garden to make it more accessible, whether your own garden or one you have inherited from someone else, identify all those aspects that you find difficult and make it a priority to change them: the beds you cannot get into to maintain, the area of lawn you cannot mow, the path that is too narrow for a barrow. If you are starting a garden from scratch, plan for accessibility, not only for today, but also to make it easier to enjoy the garden in a few years' time, when maybe you will be a little less agile.

## Paths

Paths are always difficult features to incorporate into the design of a garden. They must have a purpose, and they need to lead somewhere. But often a path is installed in the early stages, and

In square or rectangular gardens that are wide but not very deep, paths can look very contrived if they appear to be a simple route around the plot. You need either to work them through the planting, or to incorporate part of the path as a mowing strip at the edge of the lawn. If you are using gravel or paving as an alternative to grass, then the path can simply blend into this area.

the rest of the garden is built around it. This does not always mean that the path achieves its purpose or makes the garden accessible for the gardener. Long, narrow gardens often have a long, straight path down one side, ending abruptly at the end of the plot. The path needs to lead to a feature, perhaps a seat or an arbour, to make sense. It should also facilitate easy access for the mower and a wheelbarrow, and be safe to walk on in all weathers.

Whether a path is made from stone chippings, paving or bark chips, ensure that it is wide enough; remember that the width will become more restricted as the neighbouring planting develops. If you need to move a mower, barrow or wheelchair on the path, it probably should be solid; wheels do not move easily on gravel or bark. Bends in the path should be wide enough to allow you to get round them with whatever you are pushing without you having to climb into the flower bed.

## Slopes

If your garden slopes, terracing it to create level areas is the most practical solution, as these will be much easier to cultivate. Access between different levels is best provided by gentle slopes. Steep slopes can be slippery and treacherous, and as difficult to negotiate as steps. Gentle slopes are much easier, but compared to steps they take up more ground to achieve the same change in level. If you need to install a slope, seek advice from a professional landscape contractor who specializes in this type of work. If possible make any slope wide enough to accommodate two people walking side by side, or a wheelchair.

### Stepping stones

Stepping stones in grass can be a maintenance nightmare: unless you are exceptionally skilled it is difficult to get the levels just right so that you can mow over the stones, and you are likely to spend much precious time trimming around them – or regretfully leave them untrimmed. The best advice is to take them up and replace them with a suitable path.

**Top**: Broad, gentle steps are easy to negotiate. The timber sleepers give a soft and natural feel to the design.
**Above**: The slope alongside these steps makes access for a barrow or mower possible without lifting.

Stepping stones in wide flower beds and borders, however, provide easy access for maintenance. They will also allow you to get onto the beds regardless of weather and soil conditions, and you will always tread in the same place, without the risk of damage to the soil structure.

## Raised beds and planters

Raised beds have become popular in recent years, especially for the cultivation of vegetables, because they enable gardeners to provide deep, well-drained fertile soil, which most gardens lack. They also offer the opportunity to control watering and feeding and to concentrate cultivation in a manageable area.

As part of a low-maintenance garden a raised bed allows you to grow groups of plants that need a little more care and attention, ones that will not sit happily among the rough and ready rabble of the border. It will also mean you can grow diminutive plants such as alpines, which are rather more difficult to reach when planted in the border. For more on what to grow in raised beds and planters, see pages 63–64.

Raised beds can be built from bricks, concrete blocks or timber sleepers. Sectional timber kits are also readily available; these are easy to assemble and relatively economical. The width of a raised bed should be governed by how easily you can reach the centre from either side. The length is more flexible, but the bed needs to be in proportion if it is to look as if it belongs in a garden, rather than in a commercial production unit. As a general rule, a length three or four times the width is ideal.

If your raised bed is open to the ground beneath, fill it with a mixture of well-rotted manure or garden compost and good top soil. If it is on a concrete or other solid base you should treat it like a large pot or container and fill it with sterile potting compost, such as a mix of multi-purpose compost and John Innes No.3. Because regular watering will leach away nutrients, you will need to add a controlled-release fertilizer, and replenish this once or twice a year, according to what you grow.

## Consider what you grow

What you grow has a profound effect on the accessibility of the garden. Avoid plants that will grow out of reach and require regular maintenance. Vigorous climbing and rambling roses are not a good idea for those who cannot manage ladders. Wisteria falls into the same category if you are growing it as a climber;

A simply constructed raised bed softened with easy-maintenance, drought-resistant planting: sedum, nepeta, geranium and lavender.

A well-adapted small garden with raised beds and pond, seasonal planting in containers, somewhere to feed the birds, and well-planned planting for colour and interest throughout the year.

it needs pruning twice a year for best results, so you need to train it in a way that enables you to reach it easily. Taller fruit trees need pruning; this will be problematic if you are unable to climb a ladder or support a long-armed pruner.

Similarly, if you find bending difficult, avoid any low-growing plants that need regular pruning, such as roses. Choose easy-maintenance shrubs that will look after themselves (see pages 88–103).

## Moving pots and containers

Your main, permanently planted pots and containers should not need to be moved very often. Once they are in position, provided they are raised slightly above solid surfaces on pieces of tile or pot feet, they should stay put. If you do need to move larger pots, it is worth considering using small, wheeled platforms, or pot dollies. These are very popular in North America, but are not as easy to find here. However, it is worth making the effort to search out good-quality examples that move easily and are substantial enough to take the weight of filled containers.

If you must have hanging baskets or other suspended containers, either fix them at a height where they are easy to reach for watering and dead-heading, or install one of those devices that enable you to lower them to a suitable height for maintenance.

# Gardening essentials

A new garden, or a change in the way you manage your existing one, is a great opportunity to review your gardening equipment, and how and where you store it. What exactly do you need to keep the garden at its best? Is that heavy garden spade with the blister-inducing handle the most suitable tool for you to use? Could it be time to replace that lawn rake with bent and rattling tines? And do you really want to carry on with that watering can, filled in the kitchen sink?

How and where you store tools and equipment will make all the difference to your gardening life. Pile it all in the corner of a dark space at the bottom of the garden, and you are likely to think twice about going out and using it. The ideal store is perhaps a garage or utility area readily accessible from the house and the garden. Otherwise some type of garden building is the answer, again close to the house, and with plenty of racks or hooks for keeping everything in orderly fashion. This need not be a traditional shed: there are many storage chests and wall stores available that are more attractive and less obtrusive. One of these may suffice even if you have a mower since many have double doors, making access easy.

## Basic kit

All gardeners need good-quality gardening gloves. They may seem like an extravagance but most of us have experienced cheap, wet, muddy gloves on a cold winter's day – and they feel even worse the following day, when they have dried rigid. If you have roses, or a fair bit of pruning to do, consider the gauntlet-type gloves that also protect your wrists.

The next most important investment is a good-quality pair of by-pass secateurs. These are the ones that cut with a scissor action, not the ones where one blade cuts onto a broader anvil blade. Choose a pair of guaranteed quality made in Europe, not inexpensive copies from Asia. There are left- and right-handed versions, and different sizes to suit your grip – getting the right one for your hand makes all the difference. If you have difficulty cutting, especially if you have arthritic hands, secateurs with rotating handles will make the task much easier, once you get used to them. They take all the strain out of repetitive cutting.

Left: A quality wheelbarrow and a lightweight plastic lawn rake make easy work of collecting leaves – valuable compost material. Below: A neat and slender garden store that will fit into the smallest garden.

Any type of timber garden building needs to be raised off the ground to allow air to circulate and prevent damp. This means a step down into the garden. If you have a mower, it is worth putting in a concrete, paving or timber ramp: this makes life much easier when you are not feeling as energetic as you used to about cutting the grass.

Kneeling stools with high side handles make it easier to get down to the ground and back up again. Choose one with a broad, stable kneeling platform and solid handles, otherwise you will never quite feel safe when you use it.

If you find it difficult to bend, or have mature shrubs that need controlling, a good-quality pair of lightweight loppers will be invaluable. These allow you to get down into a rose bush to prune it without bending and using secateurs, and to reach up into a lilac to prune it after flowering. Various handle lengths and widths of cut are available. For cutting thicker stems, you may find loppers with an anvil action easier to use, especially those with a ratchet action, which enables you to make the cut in stages rather than in one movement.

A good plastic leaf rake will make light work of cleaning up leaves, light prunings and general garden rubbish. You will also need a stiff broom that will take stubborn litter from lawns and paving with the least amount of effort. In each case make sure the handle is comfortable and the right length for you to use without bending over.

## Tools for cultivation

The most essential digging tool is a lightweight border fork. This is ideal for digging over ground in autumn or spring, prior to planting; it is excellent for transplanting, and useful for forking over the surface of the ground between established plants. Some gardeners consider that digging with a spade does more harm than good, because of the damage that it can do to earthworms and other organisms in the soil. Digging with a conventional garden spade or fork is also much harder, especially on heavy soil because of the weight of soil you are lifting.

A traditional Dutch hoe is good for annual weed control and is efficient in beds and borders and areas covered with fine gravel. Many find

Good-quality by-pass secateurs and comfortable, durable gardening gloves are the most essential kit for any gardener.

that a long-handled weed fork is their most useful tool. It allows you to get into the beds between plants to cultivate lightly, work fertilizer into the soil and remove weeds – all without bending. A long-handled weed fork can also be used to dig small holes for planting.

Before you get too carried away buying other cultivation tools, consider an interchangeable tool system, with one or two handles and a number of different heads – a hoe, fork, leaf rake, etc. It enables you to acquire a range of useful implements as you need them, and takes up relatively little storage space.

Lastly, you need a good-quality garden trowel, with an angled neck between the blade and the handle. If the blade comes straight off the handle, the tool will have no leverage when you are trying to dig a hole or lift a small plant or a stubborn weed. Some say a trowel is an amateur's tool and not for the real gardener. This is quite untrue – no gardener should be without one. A hand fork is a matter of personal preference; this is the alternative to the long-handled weed fork for the more agile gardener.

There are a great many sets of hand-tools on the market, designed to be given as gifts. These often comprise a selection of poor-quality, impractically small tools in a 'useful and attractive' bag. They have little use in the garden and if you are unlucky enough to receive one it should be deposited in a cupboard awaiting redistribution at the next bric-a-brac sale. Never feel obliged to use one of these in an attempt to please the giver – it may result in the receipt of further useless gifts.

## Watering equipment

Using a watering can filled in the kitchen sink is not the easiest way of watering your garden. And if you decide to use a hosepipe fed out through the kitchen window you will soon find that no hose fitting has ever been made that actually fits your kitchen tap. Even if you do find one that stays in place, the chances are that it will irrigate the kitchen floor more successfully than it will water the garden.

Watering the garden in spring and summer can be therapeutic, or it can be time-consuming and laborious. The latter is invariably the case if you are not equipped for the task and have lots of plants that require irrigation at the same time. Nearly all newly planted subjects in the open ground need regular watering; once established they should require little attention, except perhaps in extreme conditions. Plants in containers and raised beds are bound to need

some regular watering throughout the year, but particularly when they are in full leaf in summer. One or two can be done with the can; more than this will require a hosepipe.

The most essential piece of watering equipment is an accessible outside tap for mains water, and a water butt, fed by the rainwater downpipe from the house roof. A good-quality hosepipe that does not kink is a must, as is a means of easy-to-use storage, such as a reel on wheels or a wall rack.

Automatic irrigation systems are available in kit form for DIY installation. They are easy to use and reliable and well worthwhile if you have a number of pots to water, providing these are grouped in one part of the garden. The most popular utilize micro-drip and spray nozzles. A simple computer control fixed to the outside tap will deliver a predetermined amount of water whenever you have set it to do so – ideal for those going away for a few days at a time. Installation is easy if you can read instructions; if you can't, ask someone else to do it for you.

Undoubtedly the most difficult containers to water are hanging baskets. A hosepipe with a long spray lance is good, but avoid any of the gadgets based on plastic bottles and pipes. The best solution of all is to stop hanging your bedding plants up in colanders to dry. Instead plant a climber to grow up the wall, and grow your bedding plants in a decent-sized pot where you can reach them with the watering can.

## Compost bins

A compost bin is essential in any garden that generates a fair amount of waste: plant clippings, light prunings, dead flowerheads, fallen leaves.

Left: An outside tap, easily accessible from the garden, takes all the effort out of watering.
Below: A watering can is essential in every garden.

Cheap hoses that kink and constantly need attention to allow the passage of water are the most frustrating timewaster in the garden. They may seem good value when you buy them, but if they are difficult to use you will avoid them and return to struggling with the watering can.

Mission control: a keen gardener will keep all his or her small garden essentials together in one place. A desk is the ideal location for seeds, catalogues, labels, string and all the rest of the paraphernalia.

Organized gardeners may use one of those garden logs, a book in which you list your plants by location, when you planted them, where you bought them, how much you paid for them, the colour of the nurseryman's eyes, etc. In reality, most of these books remain unused, destined for employment as shopping lists at a future date.

Even more organized people may retain all of this information on the computer database. Perhaps this is the future, or maybe you need a little more gardening to do ...

If your only compostable garden waste is fallen leaves in the autumn, heavy-duty refuse bags may be more practical than a bin. Collect the leaves when damp and pack them into plastic refuse bags, lightly knotting the neck of each bag when full and poking a few air holes into each with the garden fork. Then stack them up in a shady corner out of sight. In 12 months or so the leaves will be partially decomposed and at this stage they make wonderful mulch for your beds and borders.

You can also add old potting compost from containers, annual weeds (before they set seed) and of course vegetable peelings and trimmings from the house. If you have a very small garden or courtyard, a compost bin is probably not worthwhile; you would be better off recycling kitchen and garden waste through your local council green waste scheme (if there is one).

Compost containers are rarely the most attractive garden features. The best bet is a wooden slatted one with a sensible hatch or removable side to enable you to extract the compost without too much effort.

## Collecting garden waste

In a smaller garden you might find a folding, polypropylene litter bag sufficient for collecting waste. The pop-up types are ideal as after use they can be folded flat for storage. For larger gardens, a wheelbarrow is essential. Do try before you buy and never buy on price alone. Select on balance and manoeuvrability. Folding barrows, consisting of a polypropylene bag or hopper mounted on a folding wheeled frame, solve the storage problem and are ideal for light use. For heavier work, a good plastic-bodied metal-framed wheelbarrow with a broad pneumatic tyre is unbeatable. Those with two front wheels are more stable but less manoeuvrable and can only be used successfully on wide paths and level grass areas.

## Plant labels

If you are a plantaholic, and you add to your plot randomly over the year, it becomes difficult to remember what you have planted and where ... what were those bulbs you just chopped up with a trowel?

Leaving the nursery label in place, complete with colour picture, bar code and price, is a real no-no in garden design, yet a surprising number of us do this. Black labels that you scratch the name onto offer a discreet solution; attach them with soft wire or flexible plastic tie. For bulbs or perennials that die down to the ground, a label securely wired at ground level onto a stout cane is unobtrusive and effective.

For information on lawnmowers see *Keeping a lawn*, pages 16–17.

# Making the most of it

Although plants are the most important features in any garden, there are other elements that go together to create the garden picture and enable you to make the most of your outdoor living space. Most of us want somewhere to sit in the garden where we can enjoy being outside, spend time with friends and admire the results of our efforts. You probably want a bird table and birdbath to encourage wild visitors. A pot or statue will create a focal point in the picture; this may be particularly important when you look out from the sitting-room window in the evening. Taking a new look at what you want from your garden may make you think again about that greenhouse you have always wanted, or encourage you to grow a few of your own vegetables. The possibilities are endless …

A sunny terrace, surrounded by soft and fragrant planting, is just the place to sit and enjoy being in the garden. This wooden furniture is part of the picture throughout the year.

# Somewhere to sit

Above: A well-placed garden bench is welcome with all visitors to your garden. Below: A hardwood patio set can remain on the terrace all year round, ready for use whenever the sun shines.

Even in the smallest garden you need somewhere where you can perch and just enjoy being outside – somewhere to take a rest from your labours, perhaps, or to sit and chat to a visitor or relax with a cup of coffee. In the garden, however, a seat serves another purpose as well: it can be a focal point, a feature. And it conveys a message. It says: 'I enjoy spending time in my garden, I am pleased with it, I want to sit in it and admire it.'

For all these reasons, you need to consider very carefully both what you choose as a seat, and how you integrate it into the design of the garden. If you are going to sit on a garden seat, it should of course be comfortable, but comfort may be of secondary importance to appearance.

A comfortable but unattractive white plastic chair will not look appealing when viewed from the house. With just a little thought, and a few pounds, you could do so much better.

## Patio furniture

Despite the amazing range of sophisticated patio furniture on the market, many people still hang on to their odd assortment of chairs, old and ancient. These are grouped around an unsuitable table during fine spells in summer and for the rest of the year they languish with the spiders in a corner of the garage or garden shed. Perhaps now is the time to invest in a good-quality set of table and chairs that will last – furniture that can play an important role in the garden throughout the year. In our changing climate we often get lovely, bright days in autumn and early spring; if your garden furniture lives permanently outside, it is ready to be enjoyed at any moment.

If you decide to keep your table and chairs in position throughout the year, bear in mind that furniture made of wood or metal looks more at home in most gardens than that made of resin or plastic. Quality hardwood furniture can be left outside, uncovered, all year round. Either oil the wood annually to protect its colour, or allow it to bleach and go grey without treatment. This does not affect the durability of the furniture; it merely adds a pleasing maturity to its appearance.

Larger sets of wooden furniture, with more than four chairs, can look heavy and overpowering in a small space, and this is where metal comes into its own. Cast and wrought metal furniture has a very transparent quality in the garden, disappearing against the backdrop of patio stone and planting. Metal in combination with wood, ceramic, granite and marble has similarly unobtrusive qualities.

From an aesthetic point of view, you should always choose furniture that is in proportion to the size of your terrace and garden. The size of the table, of course, will depend on how many people you will usually want to seat at it, but do remember that it is more pleasant to eat at a large table than at a small one, even if there are only two of you sharing the meal. You should also select a table and chairs whose design is in keeping with the style of your garden, your house and, if it can be seen from indoors, the furniture and décor inside. A well-chosen set of furniture on the patio extends the interior of the house into the garden.

Resin-weave furniture is increasingly popular. It is made from an all-weather simulated cane bound onto a lightweight metal frame. It is comfortable and looks good in modern garden settings as well as those with a continental or oriental twist. If you do not want a conventional patio table and dining chairs, consider an outdoor sofa, armchair and coffee table. You may need to take the cushions indoors after use, but that involves little effort.

## Garden seats

If you opt for a traditional garden bench, select a good-quality one made from hardwood and stand it on paving or gravel. If you site it on the lawn, just remember that you will have to move it every time you cut the grass, and this can be laborious. It is much better to drop the

A beautiful cast-iron garden seat makes a striking feature, surrounded here by lime-green spurge and sugar-pink roses.

bench back into the border on some stone slabs for stability and surround it with planting. If this is a piece of furniture you are going to sit on and enjoy, choose one with a contoured seat and back; this will be much more comfortable and, for a short spell at least, usable without cushions. Although curved arms may look attractive, wide flat arms are useful places on which to sit a teacup or glass, if you do not have a table nearby.

There are some very pretty metal seats on the market, the light wrought type and the heavier, more ornate cast ones. These are often garden features in their own right, and sit nicely against planting or the house walls. With the addition of a cushion or two they can also be comfortable, if a little cold to sit on in the winter.

Stone seats are even colder. These can also be attractive, but they should be in keeping with other stone or paving used in the garden, as well as with the masonry of the house. They are usually made from reconstituted stone and can look rather like a concrete slab until they have mellowed and weathered. They must sit on paving slabs or gravel, and planting tucked into gaps in the paving and in the gravel really helps to soften the appearance of the stone.

## Simple seats

A seat made of a slab of wood supported on two blocks, or chunky logs or some sections of tree trunk in a group can be a nice place to perch, and also pleasing to look at. This type of seat fits well into more naturalistic planting and is a good choice in an out-of-the-way corner.

## Positioning

When positioning a seat in the garden you need to consider two main views. The first is where you will see the seat from: perhaps the windows of the house or the patio. The second is what you will see when sitting on the seat. The position will not make sense if your main view is of the compost bin or the garden shed: you need to either move the seat or make the view more interesting. This is the compromise between the functionality of the seat and its decorative qualities.

## Planting around the seat

Planting around any place you are going to sit in the garden should feature plants that you want to sit next to. Soft tactile grasses, aromatics and fragrant plants are obvious choices. In a sunny spot lavender is popular, but for something different try *Prostanthera cuneata*, the mint bush. This has tiny emerald-green leaves, crowded on compact branches, and white flowers in summer. The foliage is deliciously fresh mint fragrant. On a warm day you do not even have to touch it to smell it. *Rosmarinus officinalis* 'Green Ginger' is a lovely variety of this familiar aromatic shrub. The foliage is finer than that of many rosemaries and smells distinctly of ginger when warmed by the sun. *Hakonechloa macra* 'Aureola' is a mound-forming bamboo-like grass, with softly arching gold-streaked leaves that turn a rich corn colour in winter. It is the perfect choice to plant alongside a seat for both its colour and texture.

Thorny, spiky and prickly plants are to be avoided. Also avoid plants that drop petals that can stain clothing, and never position your

garden bench under a bird feeder for obvious reasons. If you opt for a pretty, light-coloured seat, choose plants with strong dark evergreen leaves as a background; deciduous shrubs immediately behind a wooden or light metal seat can look bare and drab in the winter. If the seat is to serve as a focal point, a yellow foliage shrub planted alongside or behind it will attract attention and highlight it as an important feature.

**Above**: A cartwheel bench sits in the lee of a wall, with perennials and grasses on either side.
**Below**: A weathered timber seat is surrounded by a swirl of pheasant's tail grass, *Anemanthele lessoniana*.

# Somewhere to shelter

This pretty arbour provides shelter from the wind and the odd light shower – a lovely spot to enjoy the garden and a good book.

Even in a small garden it is good to have somewhere where you can enjoy being outside even when the weather is less than ideal. You might like to consider an open-sided arbour, a summerhouse or a small conservatory. You might also want to think about providing some shade, to avoid having to put up a garden parasol every time you want to sit outside on a sunny day.

## Arbours

Any open-sided arbour with a roof gives shade, as well as shelter from the rain. In a small garden area, which could be part of a larger plot, this can be just a seat with a roof over it. An arbour of this type can be an attractive focal point and be the main feature in a smaller garden.

Larger arbours can accommodate a table and chairs or benches for outdoor dining. They can be open all round, or be fitted with solid panels on some of the sides to give shelter from the prevailing winds, or to screen the garden or view beyond. In some ways they are more practical than summerhouses: because they are open, they are an immediately usable part of the garden throughout the year.

## Summerhouses

The idea of a summerhouse is appealing. It offers a change of scene, somewhere to set up camp when the weather is not necessarily perfect – a little like having a beach hut on your doorstep. If well constructed and fitted with insulation and some sort of heating, a summerhouse can provide that longed-for den or study – a place of refuge for the under-gardener perhaps?

In reality many summerhouses become glorified sheds: handy storage areas for garden furniture, odd items from the house and the mower. Before you opt for a summerhouse, consider carefully how you will use it, then select one of a size and design that will enhance your garden, as well as fulfil its purpose.

## Conservatories

A well-positioned conservatory, with easy access from a key area of the house, gives you the chance to spend time in the garden whatever the weather. If you plan it well, this will be the room where you spend most of your time, winter and summer. A conservatory offers a wonderfully light environment where you can eat, read the paper, have your coffee and spend time with friends. Even a small, double-glazed conservatory will give you enough space to sit and grow a few plants, and in most small gardens is more useful than a greenhouse.

The ideal aspect for a conservatory is facing north or east. South- and west-facing conservatories can get unbearably hot in the summer, making them impossible both to live in and to grow plants in. In most conservatories you will need properly installed blinds. You will also need a source of heating, which may be independent of the home central-heating system or an extension of it.

A good conservatory is an investment and costs about the same as a home extension of equivalent size. Planning permission is usually required; the company you buy from will normally take care of this for you.

## Shade

The obvious provider of shade in a garden is a tree, but if you are planting a new tree you may have to wait a year or two for its canopy to cast enough shade.

Alternatively you could erect a pergola over part of a patio or seating area and drape it with a fast-growing climber. A fruiting vine gives a Mediterranean atmosphere when grown in this way, but it will shed its leaves in winter and it will require some pruning. The large-leaved ornamental vine *Vitis coignetiae* is a marvellous climber for providing shade. Its vigorous stems carry large, textural leaves that colour superbly in autumn. The Chinese gooseberry or kiwi fruit, *Actinidia deliciosa* (syn. *Actinidia chinensis*), is another option, with velvety, oval, pale green

leaves on twining stems. Large creamy-white flowers are produced in early summer; choose the variety 'Solo' if you want fruit. Both the vine and the gooseberry are vigorous and rampant and will require some pruning to control their size; however, their scale can be very dramatic in a small space and they impart a lush and exotic effect.

Shade sails are increasingly popular and can be used on a timber pergola, or erected on poles with guy ropes. Alternatively one end can be attached to the wall of the house, and the other supported on poles. They work well in contemporary and coastal gardens, and they provide shelter from rain as well as shade from the sun. Because shade sails put up a lot of wind resistance they must be soundly fixed to their supports. If using one with an area greater than 2sq m (20sq ft), it is advisable to have it installed professionally.

A tree is the natural provider of shade in any garden. If you are planting for shade, bear in mind that the larger the leaves, the heavier the shade the tree will cast.

Although a conservatory might take up a fair amount of your garden, because you are likely to use it as the main sitting area, you can consider it as a part of the patio. Even when the weather is good, if you can open up the doors of the conservatory to the garden, you will tend to sit under cover, rather than moving outside, especially in the evening. Furnish the conservatory as part of the garden rather than as part of the house and it will feel as if it is an all-weather garden environment, especially if you grow a few plants in it.

# Creating a fragrant bower

There is nothing more pleasant than sitting in the garden on a summer's afternoon enjoying the scents of the season. You can transform a tiny garden, or a sheltered spot in a larger plot, into a fragrant bower using a few well-chosen plants with scented flowers or aromatic foliage. Here is a suggested scheme for a sunny corner.

An arbour, gazebo, arch or small pergola could provide shelter and somewhere to sit and admire some fragrant climbers. **Roses** are an obvious choice, and there are many to choose from. *Rosa* **'Teasing Georgia'** (1) is a wonderful English rose that has flattened, many-petalled blooms of rich deep yellow with a delicious tea fragrance. It will succeed in sun or partial shade, and is free-flowering and controllable. It can be grown as a large free-standing bush or as a short climber. Unlike many climbing and rambling roses, this one bears flowers throughout the season.

Any scented garden must include honeysuckle, and *Lonicera periclymenum*

'Graham Thomas' (2) is one of the finest; with sweetly fragrant honey-coloured blooms all through summer, it is a perfect partner for *Rosa* 'Teasing Georgia'. Varieties of our native honeysuckle like this one grow on any soil in sun or shade and need little attention apart from a hard prune every few years if they get out of hand. Although without scent, a dark velvet-purple clematis such as *Clematis* 'Polish Spirit' will add to the effect and extend the season into autumn.

The mock oranges, varieties of **philadelphus**, are the most fragrant summer-flowering shrubs. Although they flower only once, in June, no garden should be without one. *Philadelphus* **'Belle Etoile'** (3) is the finest for fragrance; it has single white blooms, each with a central purple blotch and golden stamens. It grows to 3m (10ft) and tends to be upright in habit, particularly if the flowered shoots are cut back hard once the blooms have faded. Alternatively, you can be less ruthless and remove only some of the flowered shoots, using the remaining stems to support

a late-flowering climber such as *Clematis* 'Purpurea Plena Elegans'. Philadelphus are hardy and reliable and grow on any soil, including chalk.

**Pittosporums** are shrubs usually associated with foliage, but many have fragrant flowers too. The cultivars of *Pittosporum tenuifolium* have tiny chocolate blooms that often go unnoticed, apart from their scent. *Pittosporum tobira* (4) is more compact, with shining dark green leaves in whorls. Those at the end of the branches are the perfect setting for clusters of creamy, sweetly fragrant flowers; these appear in late spring and early summer and become butter yellow as they age. It likes

None of the climbers featured here looks much in the winter so it is worth adding an evergreen for year-round interest. A large-leaved ivy such as *Hedera colchica* 'Dentata Variegata' would be good. Better still, consider the lovely *Trachelospermum jasminoides*. This has small dark green, leathery leaves that turn red-green in winter. In summer the plant is studded with very fragrant, starry white flowers, like those of jasmine.

a sheltered spot, will grow in semi-shade, and makes a wonderful subject for a pot. There is also a variegated form with leaves streaked with sage green and edged with cream; its soft colours are at home anywhere.

In late summer **buddleias** are invaluable shrubs for colour and fragrance and they are magnets for colourful butterflies. Easy to grow on any soil, the only care they need is hard pruning in late winter to stimulate vigorous growth and plenty of flowers the following summer. For small gardens **Buddleja davidii 'Nanho Purple'** (5) is a good choice. It is fairly compact for a buddleia, and can be kept to 1m (3ft) in height; its branched stems carry silvery leaves and short horizontal panicles of rich purple-red flowers, whose scent is heavy and sweet.

No sunny scented spot should be without **lavender**. Fragrance is as much about foliage as it is about flowers, and lavender wins on both counts. The slender stems and delicate flowers are aromatically scented and always buzzing with bees

**Right:** Honeysuckle and roses combine above a stone seat to make a charming garden retreat.

on fine days. The silvery green foliage continues to scent the air before and after the flowers, and on well-drained soils will stay looking good throughout the winter if the plants are trimmed after flowering. There are many varieties of lavender to choose from. The deep blue, compact *Lavandula angustifolia* **'Hidcote'** (6) is still one of the finest, as is *Lavandula angustifolia* 'Imperial Gem', with rich purple flowers and more silver foliage.

To complete the picture, add a cluster of plants in terracotta pots. The leaves of some pelargoniums are wonderfully aromatic when touched. *Pelargonium* **'Attar of Roses'** (7) is a delight, with deliciously fragrant grey-green leaves and tiny pale pink flowers. Lemon verbena, *Aloysia triphylla* (8), syn. *Lippia citriodora*, is an unprepossessing little shrub with mouth-watering lemon-scented foliage. An old-

fashioned favourite, with soft, sweet perfume, is heliotrope or cherry pie; *Heliotropium arborescens* **'Chatsworth'** (9) is excellent. Just like lavish embroidery, clusters of tiny inky blue flowers crown the stems of dark green wrinkled leaves. All of these plants for pots need winter protection in a frost-free greenhouse, porch or conservatory; given this they will perform for you year after year.

# Something to look at

Garden ornaments such as statues, birdbaths, sundials and urns personalize your garden and make focal points in the garden picture. If you are downsizing and moving to a new home, perhaps some of the features of your old garden can play important roles in the new one? Their success will depend upon how you use them and integrate them into the new design.

Alternatively, you may decide to have a complete change. You may need to be ruthless and do away with that battered old urn that you bought twenty years ago for a few pounds.

That birdbath that never retained water just has to go, along with the broken statue that you tried to repair. Items like these would soon be evicted if they belonged inside the house and you were redecorating. Just because they are part of the garden you should not make do with them, especially if they do not fit into the picture you have in mind.

## Choosing a garden feature

A well-chosen object can set the scene in a small garden, or in a corner of a larger one. It can be the foundation on which you build the planting. It can clearly express the feeling or style you are trying to create, whether traditional or contemporary. It can shock, amuse, seduce or surprise but, as with a picture on the wall of your sitting room, you must like it and know that it is something you want to live with.

Garden ornaments can cost anything from a few pounds to thousands. You may find what you are looking for at a garden centre, a reclamation yard, in a magazine, on the internet or even at a car boot sale. Sometimes everyday objects like old garden tools, flowerpots or watering cans make the most appropriate features, especially if you are aiming for a traditional or nostalgic picture. At the other end of the scale, simple, contemporary sculptures are readily available in garden centres at a modest price. If you want something contemporary but with a natural feel, then look for large, smooth pebbles and pieces of slate and marble.

Statues for the garden are the most difficult things to buy. You will find a great many cast statues of identical design and varying quality. Some are based on classical designs, others on

Left: These bold vases made of layers of slate make a strong focal point amid dwarf bamboos and bergenias. A similar effect could be achieved with lighter terracotta ornaments. Below: A simple contemporary sculpture stands out against a backdrop of evergreens and herbaceous perennials.

Humorous garden statues depicting activities, sports and famous people enjoy waves of popularity. These are a matter of personal taste, and the most difficult situation arises when you are given one by a friend or relative who does not quite understand what you are trying to achieve in your garden. The only solution is to position it discreetly in a corner alongside a fairly fast-growing evergreen.

moulds that have been around for many years. If you want originality, avoid them.

## Positioning

How well any object works in a garden depends on how you position it and incorporate it into the planting. So often an ornament is marooned in an open space without any reason to be there. A birdbath in the middle of the lawn without any paving or planting not only looks deserted and lonely, it is also an obstacle to mowing and a potential hazard if the lawn is used by children and pets. Why would any bird wish to bathe in such an exposed situation, and why would you want to walk that far to fill the bath? Besides, why would you want to draw attention to the centre of an area of grass?

If the same birdbath were integrated into low planting in the foreground of the picture, perhaps on the edge of the patio, it would make more sense. You could watch the birds as they enjoy the water and you would have easy access to the birdbath to refill it. The planting would soften the edge of the patio and it would anchor the ornament into the landscape and make it a part of the garden.

The same principles apply to purely ornamental objects. A statue, or sculpture or decorative pot will unfailingly draw the eye, not only to itself but to its surroundings, so you need to be sure it is in an appropriate and attractive setting. You can also use a feature like this to draw attention away from something unsightly – the dustbin, the oil tank or the garden shed for example. Placing the ornament in the foreground will attract attention, and the eyesore will fade into the background.

## Scale and form

A small garden does not necessarily mean that you have to use small features, but the size of the object does need to be balanced by the scale of the planting. For example, a large urn surrounded by small-leaved dwarf shrubs such as thymes and hebes could look overwhelming in a small courtyard garden, particularly if the planting in the urn is also diminutive. However, the same urn could look stunning against the backdrop of the large glossy leaves of a fatsia and a large-leaved ivy, or perhaps planted with a large-leaved hosta.

Likewise, in a larger space a small ornament can become a detail feature if combined with the planting so that the two together become the focal point. Yellow leaves and white-variegated foliage are always good choices to plant alongside any ornament you want to be noticed. They highlight the object and draw attention. Any plant with foliage that contrasts in texture with its surroundings works in a similar way. Spiky plants like phormiums and bold grasses are usually effective, particularly alongside smooth, rounded shapes.

**Top:** This bright blue seat combines classic lines with modern colour, reflected in the colours of the planting. **Above:** A group of natural stones, beautifully placed, makes a thought-provoking feature on top of a low wall. **Below:** A well-weathered sundial nestles in the planting.

# Attracting wildlife to your garden

**Above:** A blackbird feasts on the ripe fruit of a rowan tree in the autumn sunshine. **Below:** Bees love the nectar-laden flowers of clovers.

Nothing brings a garden to life more than birds, bees, butterflies and other visiting creatures. Their presence is a delight throughout the year, and they play a vital role in achieving a natural balance in the garden environment. None of us likes using chemicals to control pests, so natural predators are to be encouraged. They keep the pests in check and, in return, our gardens, whether in town or country, provide welcome habitats.

A wildlife-friendly garden does not mean an untidy, unkempt plot. You do not have to restrict your planting to wildflowers and native trees and shrubs; many cultivated plants are wildlife friendly too. After all, most of us enjoy foreign food from time to time, and it is just the same with wild creatures: they quickly adapt to whatever food sources are available, enjoying many plants that have been introduced from overseas. They will help to make your garden a place that is regularly visited and inhabited by insects, birds and other animals.

## Feeding feathered friends

Not so long ago feeding the birds meant stringing up a few peanuts on cotton thread, hanging up half a coconut, or tossing stale crusts onto the lawn. Today, feeding the birds has become a national pastime, and a vast range of bird feeders and advanced feed mixes is readily available to cater for your particular bird population. A bird-feeding station or bird table is a lively focal point in the garden; watching the variety of visitors that it attracts brings hours of pleasure.

The array of choices when it comes to selecting a feeding station means you do not have to compromise appearance for efficiency. A traditional wooden bird table is only one option, and not necessarily the most cat- and squirrel-proof. Where there is a local population of feline predators, a bird-feeding station, supported by a slender metal pole, is more likely to keep the birds safe as they feed. A device of this type is unobtrusive in the garden, takes up little space and encourages the birds to feed where you can watch them easily.

Birds love somewhere to bathe, so a birdbath is an essential. Many choose a classic pedestal design, but a large saucer of water on the patio will prove just as attractive. Site your birdbath or bird table where you can see the action from indoors. A twiggy shrub or a small tree close

by will make it even more useful to birds; they love somewhere to await their turn and watch others feed.

## Plant a tree in your garden

Every garden needs a tree of some description and it is an absolute must if you are trying to encourage birds and insects. Trees provide places for birds to nest and roost. They are also the antennae of gardens, connecting them with the surrounding countryside. In urban areas, trees keep wildlife routes open, ensuring that visitors from the countryside can find their way to your doorstep and window sill.

A small tree such as a mountain ash or rowan, *Sorbus aucuparia*, is an excellent choice. It provides pleasing foliage with good autumn colour, the clusters of white flowers in spring attract pollinating insects, and hungry birds will enjoy the berries that follow in autumn and winter. Red-berried varieties are the favourites; their fruit tends to disappear before that of yellow- and white-fruited forms.

## Choose plants with single flowers

It is true that gardeners are bewitched by the flamboyance of double blooms, but it is the single flowers, allowing easy access to nectar and pollen, that are most visited by bees, butterflies and other pollinating insects. Single dahlias, for example, are showy, long-lasting summer-flowering perennials that provide us with vibrant colour, in containers and in the border, and are much appreciated by the bees. Single roses have charm and simplicity, while their central stamens are loaded with pollen and the base of each petal is rich in nectar.

The reliable potentilla is an undemanding and tough shrub with a long flowering period and buttercup-like single yellow, white, pink or orange flowers that seem magnetic to bees. It is not the most prepossessing plant in the winter, but it makes up for this with its performance in summer and autumn. Potentillas are compact and controllable enough to fit into any garden. *Choisya ternata*, the Mexican orange, has glossy evergreen foliage and clusters of single white fragrant flowers in spring and again in early autumn, making it valuable for insects at both ends of the gardening season.

## Plant a shrub that berries

Find a place for a shrub that produces berries, such as a cotoneaster, pyracantha or holly. All these not only have white flowers in spring, loved by pollinating insects, but also produce juicy red, orange or yellow berries in autumn, which are relished by the birds. They are easy to grow on any soil, in any situation.

### Trees that attract birds

*Cotoneaster frigidus* 'Cornubia'

*Cotoneaster* 'Hybridus Pendulus'

*Crataegus × persimilis* 'Prunifolia'

*Malus* 'John Downie'

*Malus × purpurea* 'Neville Copeman'

*Sorbus commixta* 'Embley'

*Sorbus* 'Joseph Rock'

**Above**: The succulent fruits of *Malus × purpurea* 'Neville Copeman' provide a real feast for birds.
**Below**: A red admiral enjoys the late summer flowers of *Choisya ternata*.

Above, left to right: *Viburnum opulus*; *Sedum spectabile* 'Herbstfreude'; a red admiral on *Verbena bonariensis*. **Below:** A brimstone on the autumn flowers of *Ceratostigma willmottianum*. **Bottom:** *Caryopteris × clandonensis* 'First Choice'.

Our British native guelder rose, *Viburnum opulus*, has white lacecap heads of flowers in spring and heavy clusters of glistening redcurrant-like fruits in autumn. It is lovely as part of a rural hedge or in a country garden. The variety *Viburnum opulus* 'Compactum' is neater and more suitable for smaller, more urban settings. *Cotoneaster franchetii* is a light, airy shrub with arching branches of grey-green leaves that carry large orange-red fruits into winter; the birds will leave them for you to enjoy in autumn, but they will soon eat them up when they get hungry later on.

## Plant late-flowering shrubs and perennials for butterflies

Many of our best-loved shrubs flower in spring so it is worth making room for later-flowering ones as these will supply welcome colour as well as providing nectar for the butterflies. Good ones include buddleia, hebe and caryopteris, hibiscus and ceratostigma.

Perennials such as *Sedum spectabile* and *Verbena bonariensis* are lovely long-blooming plants that always attract bees and butterflies. They start to flower as early as August and may still be looking good in November.

## Plant flowering aromatics

Aromatic shrubs such as lavender, thyme, sage and rosemary are ideal in sunny, dry situations, where many plants struggle to survive; their fragrant, nectar-laden summer flowers are much loved by bees and butterflies. They are excellent subjects to plant near a garden seat, where you can enjoy their fragrance and the activity of the insect visitors. They associate well with paving and gravel (see pages 20–23).

## Plant a mixed hedge

Fast-growing conifers are all too often used as hedges in urban gardens, designed to provide a near-instant barrier against the outside world. They may well succeed in this but, compared to a mixed hedge, they offer precious little to benefit visiting wildlife. When you are planting a hedge, even in a town garden, consider using a combination of deciduous and broad-leaved evergreen shrubs such as holly (*Ilex aquifolium*), guelder rose (*Viburnum opulus*), spindle (*Euonymus europaeus*) and hawthorn (*Crataegus monogyna*). All have flowers for the insects and berries and seeds for the birds. The dense, twiggy frame of a mixed hedge is a great place for birds to nest, and an excellent support for fragrant nectar-laden climbers such as our native honeysuckle (*Lonicera periclymenum*) and dog rose (*Rosa canina*).

## Make a small wildlife pond

A shallow pond with gently sloping sides is easily constructed and even something the size of a washing-up bowl provides a valuable habitat for insects such as damselflies and water boatmen, and perhaps the occasional frog. Where excavation is impossible, try a half-barrel as a pond. This can stand directly on the ground and be partially surrounded by planting or it can be sunk a little into the soil.

## Add a few wildflowers

Garden soil is often too fertile for many native, or naturalized, wildflowers; however, some will establish in just about any situation and are easy to grow from seed. Good ones for rough areas of the garden include evening primrose (*Oenothera biennis*), foxglove (*Digitalis purpurea*), ox-eye daisy (*Leucanthemum vulgare*) and comfrey (*Symphytum officinale*).

If you garden on chalk, or poor, well-drained soil, you will have more success with wildflowers naturalized in grass. This can be a way of reducing maintenance in larger gardens. Some areas of grass can be left uncut to allow the wildflowers time to develop. They must eventually be cut in late summer, and all cuttings removed, otherwise the grass will fall over and rot down in the soil; this will increase fertility, resulting in lush grass and fewer flowers.

Flowers of the cornfield, especially poppies, do not establish in grass and must be grown in an area of open ground. If you allow them to seed, disturb the ground with a fork or hoe the following spring to encourage germination.

## Do not be too tidy

Leave the seedheads of late-flowering border perennials and grasses on the plants over the winter, rather than cutting them back in the autumn: the dried stems and seedheads are decorative and many provide valuable winter food for birds. Verbascum, teasel and achillea all stay looking good into winter, and the seeds will be sought out eventually. The dry leaves of grasses such as miscanthus are often used by early nesting birds.

An undisturbed corner of the garden, perhaps with a few logs or some old clay pots, can be a refuge for many creatures. Even those less appealing insects that live under stones have their role to play in the garden environment, so it is worth providing the facilities that will encourage them to stay.

**Above**: Poppies and cornflowers, wildflowers of the cornfield, need disturbed soil to thrive.
**Below**: A damselfly rests on the edge of a pot. **Bottom**: Seedheads of globe thistle left in the border.

# Water – the magic ingredient

**Left**: Still water brings an extra level of interest to the garden; it also enables you to grow some wonderful plants, including exquisite water lilies.
**Below**: A narrow, shallow pool, lush planting and a lead heron create the effect of a natural stream.

Water brings a garden to life. Whether still or moving, it attracts attention and adds another dimension to the design of the garden. A small pool or a self-contained water feature is simple to install and does not need to take up a lot of room. Whatever the size of your plot, it is worth considering water either as a principal feature or as a design detail.

## Simple moving water

In recent years the small, moving water feature has become an essential ingredient in garden design. You may feel that you have spent too many hours watching makeover programmes on television, waiting for its arrival: the 'washing-up bowl' with a lid, ceremoniously sunk into the ground beneath a mound of pebbles over which water pours noisily and ungracefully until the sump dries up.

Do not be put off: it does not have to be like this. A small, well-installed, self-contained pebble fountain can produce the gentle sound of running water that will cut out traffic noise and the neighbour's radio, turning your garden into an oasis of calm.

The secret of success is to use a large, good-quality sump (bowl with lid) and a reliable pump. Never use the cheapest pebble pool available; these rarely hold sufficient water and have flimsy lids incapable of supporting the pebbles. Choose a pump that is larger than the minimum size needed for the pool, and one that can be regulated to produce the required flow. This will not have to work as hard to pump the water, so it should last longer and be capable of continuous use. Do not worry if none of this makes sense – visit a reputable dealer and take advice. All you should have to do after installation is to keep the sump topped up with water, and occasionally clear away any fallen leaves.

You will of course require a power supply, which must be installed by a qualified electrician. The days of pushing an electric cable through a buried hosepipe are over! Once you have a properly installed power source you could also consider introducing some simple garden lighting. This will bring the water and surrounding planting to life when darkness falls, and will enable you to enjoy the garden from the house in the darker evenings of autumn and winter. Even the most basic low-voltage lighting kit can be very effective.

## Still water

Even if the thought of electricity and sumps puts you off, there is still no need to dismiss the idea of water altogether. Still water, even if only in the form of a tiny pool, can be just as effective. Still water reflects the sky and surroundings, so it appears to move and change with the light. It adds great depth to the garden picture and in doing so it can make a small space seem larger.

Water combines well with the paving of a terrace, either in the form of a narrow rill, or as a small square or rectangular pool. The most important thing to remember is that the surface of water is always dead level – if the paved area slopes, the water will not slope with it and the pool will sit awkwardly.

More informal pools can be set on the edge of planted areas or into areas of grass or gravel. The secret of success is to hide the edges of the liner carefully, as pieces of butyl rubber showing around the pool will spoil the effect.

It is a good idea to construct at least one side of the pool as a gently shelving beach; this allows wildlife access to drink and serves as an escape route for any careless creatures that fall in.

A raised pool brings the water closer. The broad stone edge is a handy place to perch and enjoy the plants and fish at close quarters.

## Raised pools

If excavating a hole to create a pond is beyond you, then consider an above-ground pool, built from bricks, blocks or timber sleepers, and lined with butyl. You must remember that the supporting walls will have to withstand considerable pressure from the water within, so these will have to be secure, and tied in to one another at the corners. A well-constructed raised pool, with substantial walls and a broad coping around the top, can make an ideal place to sit or perch in the garden. If you

Raised pools are more accessible than sunken ones because they bring the water level closer to you, making aquatic life more visible and easier to reach whenever maintenance is required. They are also safer if children or pets use the garden.

patio container, especially if grouped with other pots permanently planted with shrubs like acers, azaleas, pieris and phormiums.

## Fish and plants

If you want to keep fish in a pond then it needs to be large enough – at least 1m (3ft) in diameter – and deep enough – at least 60cm (2ft) deep in milder areas, 1m (3ft) elsewhere. The minimum size would allow you to keep three or four small goldfish. If you have not had aquatic livestock before, goldfish are the best choice: they are hardy and reliable and do not require the deep, filtered water demanded by Koi carp and other fancier fish. Bear in mind that if you do have goldfish, you may find you will not get frogs or newts.

More importantly, a still pond enables you to grow aquatic plants: water lilies, irises, rushes and a host of other beauties that naturally grow in water. Even a smaller pool will accommodate a water lily if you choose one of the pygmy varieties and site your pond in an open sunny position away from overhanging trees.

Choose varieties that are the right size for your pond. Water lilies and marginal plants like irises are best grown in soft fabric containers, rather than in plastic baskets with hessian liners. These are less obvious in the pool, and you can turn down the edges if necessary, to make sure they are beneath the surface of the water. Always use proper aquatic soil, and cover the surface with gravel. If you choose the right plants and plant them correctly, they should remain happy for several years without the need to lift them from the pool, divide and replant them. This is heavy, awkward work and should be avoided.

**Top**: Goldfish add movement and colour to a pond. **Above**: Three ceramic bowls of water and a dwarf bamboo create an oriental effect. **Below right**: Emerging water irises.

When planting a pond, think carefully about the plants you choose. Many people go wrong by accepting gifts from other pond owners. As soon as a friend tells you that he or she has a mass of irises, or the water lilies have gone mad, the alarm bells should start to ring. This means that the plants on offer may be far too vigorous for your pond and will quickly take over.

construct on flat, solid ground, and the walls do not require foundations. (Take care if you use treated sleepers, as they may seep tar.) The edges of the liner are easily concealed under timber coping around the top of the pool.

On a smaller scale, a raised pool can be made in a large ceramic or plastic bowl. These are popular elsewhere in Europe but not widely available in the UK, so you may have to do some research in order to find one. Planted with one or two slower-growing water plants, such a pool can make an excitingly different

# Plants for small ponds

There are a great many plants suitable for small ponds and patio pools. Here are a few good ones to get you started.

## 1 *Aponogeton distachyos*

Water hawthorn is a fine alternative to a water lily in a small pond. The oval green floating leaves are virtually evergreen and the vanilla-scented, white and black flowers – which are rather like those of broad beans – are produced at any time of the year. An established plant is rarely without flowers.

## 2 *Butomus umbellatus*

The flowering rush is a British native with very narrow grass-like leaves reaching 60cm (2ft) or more. The delicate rose-pink flowerheads arrive in early to midsummer and are held high above the leaves. It is graceful, beautiful and not greedy on space.

## 3 *Iris sibirica* 'Silver Edge'

This lovely narrow-leaved iris grows happily as a border perennial in fertile soil that is not too dry. It is equally happy in shallow water, only 2cm (¾in) deep over the planting container. Compact and well behaved, it grows to 60–90cm (2–3ft) high. The exquisite violet-blue flowers, with a silver edge to the ruffled petals, appear in June.

## 4 *Nymphaea* 'Pygmaea Helvola'

This is one of the smallest water lilies, with tiny olive-green leaves and starry, pale yellow flowers in summer. It will grow in small ponds as long as there is at least 15cm (6in) of water over the planting container. It does not require much soil, so roll over the edge of the planting bag to create a shallow bowl.

For a small pool over 60cm (2ft) deep, the old varieties *Nymphaea* 'Marliacea Rosea', with glowing pink flowers, and *Nymphaea* 'Marliacea Chromatella', with soft yellow flowers and copper-marbled foliage, are reliable choices. Although these are more vigorous than the miniatures, their growth is restricted in shallow water.

There are many varieties of water lily available, both new and old, from specialist water-plant growers. Hampton Court Palace Flower Show, held in July each year, is a favourite venue for some of these nurseries to exhibit their plants and this is a good place to see and buy them.

## 5 *Stratiotes aloides*

The water soldier is a fascinating floating plant that needs no container: just drop it into the water. It sinks to the bottom in winter and rises to the surface in summer. With its narrow, sword-shaped leaves, it resembles a yucca or aloe in the water; small creamy-white flowers form at the base of the leaves in summer. It multiplies over the years: when you get too many, fish them out and add them to the compost heap.

# Some gardening still to do

**Left**: A greenhouse is a place for gentle pottering, whatever the weather. **Top**: A glorious bougainvillea needs only some winter warmth. **Above**: Exotic orchids are within your reach, even in a small greenhouse.

Just because you are downsizing, or at least making the garden easier to manage, it does not mean that you want to give up gardening altogether. No matter how small your plot, or how carefully you plan it for low maintenance, rest assured there will still be some work for you to do.

No garden stands still: both plants and weeds continue to grow. Some plants need replacing after a few years, and there is always tidying, sweeping and dead-heading to keep the garden looking its best. However, most of us want a little more than maintenance work; we want to have some fun in the garden, a few challenges and the opportunity to develop our skills, no matter how long we have been gardening.

## A small greenhouse

A greenhouse can bring a great deal of pleasure and means you can potter among your plants even when it is cold or wet. On a sunny winter's day the temperature under glass soon rises, and even when a chill spring wind is blowing the greenhouse offers a warm place to shelter.

A greenhouse provides a place to overwinter tender patio plants such as cannas, callas, pelargoniums and fuchsias. All you need to do is lay on sufficient heat to keep it frost-free. Alternatively, you could leave it unheated and use it to grow interesting alpines, pots of early bulbs and perhaps a lemon tree to supply you with fresh fruit for your gin and tonic. For the more enthusiastic greenhouse gardener, a heating system that will raise the minimum

Good housekeeping is essential in a greenhouse, not only for the health of the plants but also for the appearance of the greenhouse itself. This is not the place to store unsightly equipment, faded packets of fertilizer and bottles of garden chemicals. This is the place to show off your horticultural skills and those tender treasures you nurture under glass.

night temperature above 10°C (50°F) will enable you to grow orchids and a wide range of more exotic subjects. For those who just enjoy the pleasure of growing things, a greenhouse is the place to raise seeds, root cuttings, and experiment. Even if you do not have room for the resulting progeny in your own garden, others will have.

So a greenhouse is a huge asset, and it seems a waste just to grow tomatoes and the odd cucumber in summer. An empty greenhouse in winter is rarely a pretty sight, and in a small garden is especially noticeable.

A utilitarian greenhouse is unlikely to enhance a garden, especially if it is clearly visible from the house. If you are considering erecting one in a new garden then buy a good-quality, well-designed and pleasing structure and site it close to the house, where you will find access easy all year round. Make sure you install a water supply and a power supply at the outset. You also need to think about shading: blinds are not the cheapest way to shade a greenhouse but they are certainly easier than having to apply liquid shading to the glass every spring and remove it every autumn.

One thing you have to remember with a greenhouse is that it cannot be left unattended when plants are in growth in spring and summer. You might be able to leave it for a few days in winter but, when temperatures start to climb, plants under glass will not survive without water and ventilation.

## Raised beds

Raised beds are popular with gardeners of all ages for the cultivation of vegetables. You can grow a range of different varieties in a small

Even a low raised bed makes maintenance easier and brings your plants that little bit closer; the drainage is good too.

Whatever your soil, a raised bed gives you control over the growing conditions and ensures good drainage. The great advantage of a raised bed is that you do not have so far to bend to reach your plants. If you construct it from solid timber sleepers it will have thick walls that you can probably perch on while working; be careful if you use recycled sleepers treated with creosote, as in warm weather these may seep tar, which will stain clothing.

Top: *Zauschneria californica* 'Dublin' is a dwarf sun-loving shrub, ideal for a raised bed with a gravel mulch. Centre: *Rhododendron* 'Horizon Monarch' is one of many acid-lovers that a gardener on chalk could grow in a raised bed with lime-free soil. Above: Agapanthus love sun and the good drainage that a raised bed or a container offers.

space and, providing you site the bed in an open, sunny position and fill it with a good-quality growing medium, you will get excellent results. A good choice of compost would be a soil-less multi-purpose compost mixed with John Innes No.3. The latter is loam based so gives the growing medium more weight and helps retain water and nutrients. If the raised bed sits on a soil base, you can use a mixture of top soil and garden compost. In either case, you will need to feed regularly with a slow-release general fertilizer. Those gardening organically should consider fish, blood and bone.

You can also use a raised bed to grow those little gems of plants that tend to get lost in the border; if you have difficulty bending, they may in any case have become far beyond your reach. Alpines, dwarf bulbs and hellebores are just a few examples; dwarf shrubs such as helianthemums and ericas and dwarf slow-growing conifers are other possibilities. Mulching the surface of the bed with grit or gravel shows off the plants, and keeps winter wet away from the foliage.

Alternatively, a raised bed makes it possible to grow plants that will not succeed on your garden soil. Although most plants will grow on most soils, ericaceous plants such as rhododendrons, azaleas, pieris and camellias will not grow on chalk or alkaline soils. Now there is one thing that is certain: a gardener may never have had the desire to grow ericaceous plants, but once he or she has a garden on chalk soil, an overwhelming urge to grow rhododendrons and camellias will take over. This usually results in an initial attempt at planting some unfortunate specimen in the open ground and drenching it regularly with sequestered iron. As the plant gradually takes on a more yellow hue and growth becomes more stunted, alternative solutions are sought. A raised bed filled with lime-free compost is the answer. Again, use a mixture of soil-less ericaceous compost and lime-free John Innes.

## Pots and containers

These are a part of the garden that needs regular attention, particularly if you use seasonal bedding plants. A few well-selected containers make a real impact and by varying the planting you can change the look of the garden twice a year if you want to. Choose large containers and fill them with good-quality potting compost. The taller the pots, the less bending you will need to do.

When your enthusiasm for bedding wanes, perhaps along with the energy needed to replant them, you can exchange the seasonal planting for permanent subjects (see *Pots and containers*, pages 136–137). Many shrubs can live happily in pots for years providing you supply some slow-release fertilizer and water them regularly. Even then you can keep one or two containers

to fill with spring-flowering bulbs and a few pelargoniums for summer colour. Growing in containers is a good way of regulating the amount of gardening you have to do; the one thing you have to consider is who will water them if you are away.

## Buy something that you do not know how to grow

From the time we first start gardening we all love the challenge of finding out how to grow a plant and how to make it thrive in our care. Those who claim that we all want gardening to be as easy as possible, and that we want only plants that need no care and attention, should take a look at recent fashions in the plant world: tree ferns, for example, or bananas from seed. How many of us have brought some seeds of an exotic plant back from holiday, and done our best to grow them here? We know that we may have little chance of success, but it does not stop us trying.

If you ever need to rekindle your passion for plants, go out and buy something you know nothing about. An exotic perhaps, an unusual bulb or some seeds that look difficult to grow. We are very fortunate today that we have such an incredible range of plants to work with, both established favourites and new introductions. For this reason alone there will always be some gardening still to do!

Far left: *Pelargonium* 'Vancouver Centennial' is shown off beautifully by an oxblood glazed pot. Left: This bonsai larch will be happy in this pot for many years.
Below left: *Aeonium* 'Zwartcop', a sun-loving succulent, and *Amicia zygomeris* (below), from Mexico, are examples of the many exciting plants that could give you the opportunity to try something new.

If you are not already a member, consider joining your local gardening club or horticultural society; there are literally hundreds across the country. They organize a variety of speakers, visits and events during the course of the year, and they give you the opportunity to meet other gardeners, who are likely to have faced exactly the same challenges. Gardeners are sociable people, and meeting folk with the same interest is always stimulating. If you live alone, a gardening club is often a great source of assistance with those jobs you cannot manage yourself. This may also be a good place to meet gardeners who can look after your plot while you are away, particularly if you enter into a reciprocal arrangement.

There are many societies that concentrate on a particular group of plants: fuchsias, orchids, alpines, pelargoniums, for example. The membership is rarely made up purely of experts; it is usually a mix of keen plantsmen and women and gardeners with an interest. Joining one of these groups may be just the way to give your hobby a new dimension.

# Growing vegetables

There is no doubt about it, growing vegetables can be hard work. If you have had a vegetable plot at any time, you will realize that it needs a fair amount of commitment in terms of time and energy throughout most of the year. Is it worth it?

From a financial point of view the answer is no; but for the satisfaction of picking your own produce fresh from your garden, perhaps the answer is yes. Knowing precisely what chemicals and fertilizers have – or have not – been used on the food you eat is an added incentive to grow your own, however small your garden.

If you are downsizing and will have no room for a dedicated vegetable patch, you may still wish to grow a few tomatoes or runner beans, or a few leaf or root vegetables among the flowers. If you have no space for vegetables in the open ground, then you can successfully grow them in pots, cropping bags and raised planters (see page 36).

## Growing tomatoes

A home-grown tomato, picked fresh from the vine, has such a superior flavour to a chilled supermarket fruit that it really is worth the effort, despite the fact that tomatoes are one of the trickiest crops to grow.

Tomatoes can be conveniently grown in growbags in a sunny corner of a patio. This may well give excellent results, but it is not the most attractive way to present them. Even good-quality growbags are made of brightly coloured polythene that will stick out in the garden like a sore thumb. Growbags were originally developed for use in commercial glasshouses; because they are replaced at the end of each growing season, they do away with the need to sterilize the soil to prevent soil-borne pests and diseases. From commercial production they found their way into the domestic greenhouse and then onto the patio. Because growbags are so widely used, gardeners have almost come to believe that you cannot grow tomatoes in anything else. There are other ways.

If you want the plants to look at all attractive, grow them in terracotta flowerpots filled

Carrots, beetroot and radishes can be grown in patches in beds and borders between shrubs and herbaceous perennials. Cultivate the ground thoroughly, then broadcast sow the seed, scattering it thinly over the surface. Cover with a thin layer of multi-purpose compost and keep well watered. Thin the seedlings according to the instructions on the packet to give the vegetables space to develop.

**Above**: Tomato 'Tumbling Tom' produces small sweet fruits on compact plants that will trail over the edge of a pot or cascade from a hanging basket. **Left**: Tomatoes and chillies in terracotta pots make an attractive feature on the patio and produce a good crop of tasty fruits.

When you are growing tomatoes in containers, make sure you water them regularly but take care not to give them too much; allow the compost to become dry to the touch before watering again. Once the first tiny green fruits appear, start regular feeding with a liquid tomato food.

with John Innes No.3 compost or a multi-purpose compost containing John Innes. Choose traditional pots, around 40cm (16in) in diameter, and grow one plant in each.

This also overcomes the problem of support often encountered when using shallow growbags. When you plant out your tomatoes in mid-May, put a stout bamboo cane in place beside each plant. Alternatively you can use spiral metal plant supports. These were originally developed for use with tomatoes; they look good and they work efficiently.

## Other fruiting crops

You can grow aubergines, peppers and chillies in exactly the same way. Chillies can be grown in slightly smaller pots, as they make squatter, bushier plants. Group the pots together and mix them with containers of brightly coloured seasonal bedding plants, such as gazanias, French marigolds, nasturtiums and pelargoniums, and you will have an attractive feature in the garden, rather than a production area that is tolerated because it produces a few worthwhile fruits.

## Essential beans

Runner beans are one of the most difficult vegetables to give up if you have been used to growing them in your vegetable garden. They are a seasonal delight, and should be treated as such. Despite numerous methods suggested for freezing beans, they never taste the same as the freshly picked product, and frankly commercial producers do a better job at freezing vegetables. By growing a few bean plants in a large container or among the flowers, you should have just enough to enjoy in season – and there

will be no pressing obligation to freeze or make chutney with any surplus.

If you want to grow traditional climbing runner beans, you need a large container of sufficient depth to support a wigwam of leaves. A half-barrel is ideal, or a large pot at least 60cm (2ft) in diameter. Fill the container with good-quality multi-purpose compost with

**Above:** Chilli 'Apache' produces profuse, small hot fruits over a long period from late summer into autumn. Grown in a container it can be brought into a conservatory or greenhouse, where it will continue to fruit until midwinter.

**Below left:** For runner beans to set well you must keep them well watered once they start to flower.

The key to success with beans in pots is to water regularly; never let them dry out. Pick the beans often and pick them young to enjoy them at their best.

**Above:** You can find room for a few runner beans in any garden.
**Right:** Potatoes grown in a potato bag take up little space and give excellent results.

In damp seasons, potatoes often suffer from blight, a disastrous fungal infection. To avoid this, grow only early varieties; plant them early and harvest them in June, before blight becomes an issue.

added John Innes, then put a wigwam of six or eight canes, at least 2m (6ft) tall, in position before you plant.

Any potting compost contains only enough nutrients for the first six weeks of growth; after that you need to supplement with a fertilizer. Before you plant your beans in a container add a generous handful of controlled-release fertilizer to the compost; this should supply sufficient nutrients for most of the growing season.

In early May plant one runner bean plant next to each cane. Alternatively sow two seeds directly into the container beside each cane; after germination, remove the weaker seedlings to leave one strong plant by each cane. There are many varieties to choose from: 'Red Rum' is a good red-flowered bean as it is self-fertile and crops reliably. White-flowered varieties set more easily in a difficult season, but they are not the most attractive. 'Painted Lady' has wonderful bi-coloured red and white flowers and is a good choice for the patio, as is 'Sunset', with lovely salmon-pink blooms.

If you do not have the space for climbing runner beans, then try one of the bush varieties. 'Hestia' is particularly attractive, with red and white blooms on bushy plants that can produce a prolific crop of tasty beans. Bush runner beans can be grown in smaller pots, as long as these are larger than 30cm (12in) in diameter. Five plants in a 45cm (18in) pot would be ideal to produce a useful crop for one person.

French beans can be grown in pots in exactly the same way. The climbing French bean 'Blue Lake' is justifiably popular for its rounded succulent pods of delicious flavour. Although its leaves are large, the stems are light and twining, so plants are easier to support than are most climbing runner beans.

## Potatoes in containers

Whether you have space in the open ground or not, growing early potatoes in containers is well worthwhile. It avoids all that ground preparation and earthing up, and a disappointing harvest will be a thing of the past. Potato bags (readily available in garden centres) provide a cube of compost 60cm (2ft) deep and square, enough for three to five tubers to grow and produce a crop of nice, clean potatoes that are worm-hole free and need little preparation before cooking. Alternatively you can use a large plastic pot.

Plant your seed potatoes in March or early April. Position three to five tubers on 20cm (8in) of compost at the bottom of the container and cover them with a similar depth of compost.

Once the shoots have emerged, cover them with more compost. Repeat this until the container is nearly full, keeping the compost moist. When the haulms (stems and leaves) are fully developed, and ideally the plants have flowered, explore the compost in search of tubers. If you want only a few at a time you can harvest repeatedly like this. Otherwise, tip the whole lot out and retrieve your bounty in one go. Varieties such as 'Charlotte' and 'Duke of York' are particularly delicious grown in this way.

## Salad leaves and herbs

When it comes to home-grown lettuces, either your plot will be awash with them or you will have only those bolted, slug-ridden ones we are all determined to eat, just because we have grown them. Cut-and-come-again varieties are good to grow if you want only small amounts of salad leaves at one time. They can be rather soft and bland in flavour and texture, but if you combine them with home-grown rocket and flat-leaved parsley, they are transformed into the best of the salad crops.

If you grow only one salad leaf in the garden, grow rocket. It is flavoursome, easy, and quick

to mature – and expensive to buy at the supermarket. Ignore the instructions on the seed packet and sow at any time in a sheltered spot in well-drained soil; alternatively grow it in a large pot of multi-purpose compost near to the walls of the house.

If you use fresh herbs and buy them from the supermarket, you will realize that these are often the most expensive cooking ingredient for their volume and weight. Most herbs are easy to grow in the garden, in pots on the patio, or on the window sill. Some, such as thyme, rosemary and sage, are best bought as plants; you probably only want one plant to supply a reasonable crop. Others such as parsley, chives and basil are easily raised from seed, especially if you have a sunny window sill. Basil is not frost hardy and will cope outdoors only after the end of May; even then, it will need a warm, sheltered position.

**Above left**: Early potatoes such as 'Charlotte' produce a good crop when grown in a growbag.
**Above**: Rocket is quick to grow, easy and delicious picked fresh from the garden. **Below**: Pots of essential herbs look great on a sunny patio and produce a useful crop of fresh leaves for kitchen and barbecue.

# Growing fruit

Those with space may be tempted by the idea of planting fruit trees for the grandchildren. In reality, by the time the trees start to fruit the grandchildren have usually lost interest in the wonderful world of gardening, and moved on to other more trendy things. You are left with the mini orchard to maintain – and possibly a glut of fruit to pick and deal with.

The idea of picking your own fruit fresh from the garden may seem appealing but, as with vegetables, growing fruit takes a good deal of time and energy. The solitary apple tree is as much a part of the English garden as a rose or lavender bush, but it does need care and attention, particularly in a small garden. Trained fruit is fashionable and looks good in pictures, but can you keep it looking just as attractive on your plot?

## Fruit trees

Unless you are really set on the idea of planting a fruit tree, think again if you are looking towards low-maintenance gardening. Apples and pears need regular pruning if they are to perform well and enhance the garden. At some point in their life they will suffer from disease, and their foliage is unexciting at the best of times. The blossom is lovely in spring and the fruit can be very attractive, but for an ornamental tree you could do better.

Plums and cherries can be even more problematic and the trees are even less attractive. If you envisage a pretty cherry tree laden with succulent fruits, think again. The tree is more likely to be smothered with blackfly at the tips of every shoot, and swarming with blackbirds as soon as the fruits ripen – if you get any you will be lucky. Plums can be productive, if you keep the wasps at bay, but the blossom is short-lived and the foliage dull and lifeless.

If you must have an apple or a pear, buy a bush tree: one that branches from 1m (3ft) or so above the ground. This means the head of the tree is easy to reach, and so the fruit is easy to pick. If possible, choose one with a semi-dwarfing rootstock, such as MM106 for apples (you rarely have a choice of rootstock for pears); trees using any of the more dwarfing rootstocks can be weak, and must be kept staked throughout their lives.

If you do not have other apples or ornamental crabs close by for pollination, Apple 'Cox's

'Selfing' is a good choice. It produces some fruit on its own, without the need for a pollinating partner, and is not too vigorous. Likewise, Pear 'Conference' is self-fertile and does not need another variety for pollination.

Trained fruit in the form of espaliers, fans and cordons can look very attractive if immaculately maintained. Plant a good specimen at the outset and grow it against a wall or fence at least 2m (6ft) high; make sure this is properly wired beforehand, to enable you to tie in the growth as the tree develops. Consult a good book on growing and training fruit.

Step-over fruit trees, trained as low boundaries to beds and borders, are often glamorized in magazines. They may seem a convenient way of growing fruit, especially if you are short of space, but to keep them productive and looking good you must be prepared to put in a great deal of hard work, involving a lot of bending.

## Soft fruit

Currants should be low on your list of priorities. They have a relatively short season, take up lots of space for the size of crop they give, and the birds are likely to eat more of them than you

do. If you do grow one, perhaps on a corner of the vegetable plot if you have one, grow a redcurrant or a dessert gooseberry. These require less attention and pruning than blackcurrants do, and even a few berries are worthwhile. If you do not get around to picking them, the birds will appreciate them anyway.

Raspberries do need a bit of space, but they suit shadier areas of the garden because of their woodland origin. The best to grow are the autumn-fruiting varieties, which fruit on the current year's wood. These are simply cut down to the ground in winter and the new canes start to fruit in late summer, continuing well into autumn. 'Autumn Bliss' is an excellent and well-proven variety. The new variety 'Polka' promises to be just as good.

## Fruit worth growing in a small plot

If you are dedicated to home production, there are some fruits that are worth growing in a small garden. These are the lower-maintenance options and ones where even a small crop justifies the time and effort you put in.

To get an even longer season from your autumn-fruiting raspberries leave some of the canes after fruiting, rather than cutting them down in winter. These will produce berries the following midsummer, and new canes will still develop alongside them to continue the season into autumn. Cut the older canes down to the ground once they have finished fruiting.

**Top left**: Pear 'Conference' grown against a wall produces lovely fruit. **Top right**: Autumn-fruiting raspberries bear delicious fruit over a period of several weeks. **Left**: Flavour-filled redcurrants look attractive and need little attention.

Above: Blueberries are easy to grow in a pot, or in the open ground if you have acid soil. Below right: A strawberry pot makes an attractive feature anywhere in the garden.

Alpine strawberries are rampant ground-cover plants and may be considered invasive in some gardens. However, in the semi-shade under mature shrubs they do a good job suppressing weeds and produce delicious little fruits. With their bright green leaves, white flowers and scarlet mini strawberries, they have a lot going for them.

## Blueberries

Blueberries have become very popular in recent years. The firm purple-black berries are appealing to look at, aromatic and delicious and, we are promised, so good for us that we will live forever if we eat them! In the garden the plants are attractive shrubs that require little attention and they have good foliage that colours well in autumn. However, they are ericaceous and need acid soil. If you do not have this, you can grow them just as successfully in pots.

Use large, deep flowerpots, ones that do not narrow at the neck, to make it easier to extract the plants if you need to re-pot them. Plant in lime-free John Innes compost, and position the pots in sun or semi-shade. Keep them well watered throughout the season, and feed annually in spring with a slow-release ericaceous fertilizer. Blueberries need no regular pruning, but they do benefit from light pruning after fruiting to keep the plants in shape.

There are a number of good varieties widely available, including 'Jersey', 'Blue Crop', 'Duke' and 'Spartan'. Although most are self-

fertile to some extent, you will get a better crop if you have two or more different varieties that will fertilize one another. Choose those that mature at different times to prolong the cropping period. Grow one plant in each pot and group two or three pots together.

## Strawberries

Strawberries are widely available and inexpensive in season, but they taste so much better if picked fresh from the garden when warmed by the sun. Strawberries do particularly well in pots and containers because they like good drainage; also, the fruits are not splashed with soil or nibbled by slugs, so remain clean and intact.

is striking and ornamental and makes an impact in any garden.

The secret of success with a fig is to contain the roots. Grow it in a large tub against a wall or plant it in a container with the bottom taken out, plunged into the ground alongside a wall or a fence. If you bend the branches over in the early stages, and tie them to wires on the wall or fence, this will restrict growth and encourage fruiting. Hard pruning should be avoided as this promotes vigorous growth.

The variety 'Brown Turkey' is the most widely planted, but many other figs are now offered as container-grown plants.

**Above left:** Growing strawberries in a pot keeps the ripening fruit off the ground and away from slugs.
**Above:** Figs usually start to ripen in late summer.
**Left:** Growing a fig in a container restricts its growth and helps to encourage fruiting.

Buy pot-grown plants in autumn or early spring and grow them in large pots, cropping bags or strawberry barrels. Traditional terracotta strawberry pots with side planting holes look good but do need very regular watering. Place containers in sun or partial shade, and remember to cut back the foliage after fruiting to encourage new leaves to grow.

Strawberry plants produce runners: young plants on the end of horizontal stems. Some of these can be potted up to fruit the following year. But it is important not to hang on to your plants for too long: their performance gradually deteriorates as a result of viral diseases and other afflictions. Keep them for three years, then dispose of them and buy some new ones. Seed-raised strawberries are becoming more popular; the plants have vigour and establish quickly when planted out.

## Figs

Fig trees are vigorous plants that are easy to grow, like poor, well-drained soil, and thrive in a sunny situation. Their deeply lobed foliage

In mild areas figs need no attention. In colder areas the embryo fruits, present on the plants in winter, are often damaged by frost and they never reach maturity. If this is a problem in your garden, remove any embryo fruits that are larger than a pinhead in February, so that the plant will not waste energy in developing them. The remaining, really tiny fruits will then develop to mature in early autumn.

# The planting picture

Ultimately the look of your garden is the result of how you put the plants together to create the picture. Do not just think of your plot as a patch of ground; think of the whole space vertically and horizontally – see it as a canvas. Consider how you will add colour, form and texture to create interest across the whole picture, and throughout the year. Looking at the garden in this way helps you to balance colours and to achieve the right proportions of planting and open space. If you do this you will be well on your way to a pleasing result.

A bold drift of hostas, sprinkled with dainty dicentras, shows how effective a simple scheme can be. The variety of colour in the hostas emphasizes the value of foliage.

# Planting layers and proportions

Whatever the size of your garden, the effect is more pleasing if there is something of interest at every level of the planting picture, from the ground right to the height of the tree-tops. This is what we find in the most appealing natural landscapes: they feel friendly and comfortable and we want to spend time in them. Space is also an important consideration: striking the right balance between the amount of planting and open space will make all the difference not only to how the garden looks, but also to how pleasant it feels to be in.

## High-level interest

In a small garden it is particularly important to include height – that is, interest above eye level – to make the space three-dimensional and to increase the planting area vertically. If you ignore height, you run the risk of the garden being flat and uninteresting; it will also appear smaller. A small tree, a bamboo, a pergola, a tall shrub or a climber on an obelisk are all ways of adding height.

## The eye-level view

The layer of planting at eye level is equally important. This should be the main area of structural planting in the garden, as it will be viewed throughout the year, not only from within the garden itself but also from the ground-floor windows of the house. Well-chosen shrubs, with interesting form and leaf colour and texture, are what deliver here. Seasonal interest and variety is added with tall perennials and climbers. This is also a level where the bark of a tree can make a major impact; be sure to take this into consideration when making your selection.

## Nearer the ground

The layer of planting nearest to the ground, in other words below eye level, is the easiest to influence and change fairly regularly. Usually there is no shortage of interest here because this is where we do most of our gardening work. Perennials, dwarf shrubs, bulbs and bedding plants all play their part. If you want to spend less time gardening, you should increase the number of dwarf evergreens you have in this layer to create effective ground cover.

**Left:** Interest at all levels is centred on a phormium in a pot and an old cartwheel. This strong focal point in the foreground makes the space seem more three-dimensional.
**Below:** *Betula utilis* var. *jacquemontii* 'Grayswood Ghost' is a graceful birch that adds height without density.

Light height is particularly useful in the foreground, enhancing perspective and making the space seem bigger. Airy grasses such as *Deschampsia cespitosa*, and tall slender perennials such as *Verbena bonariensis* and *Gaura lindheimeri* work brilliantly here as they create a softly moving curtain between you and the garden beyond.

## How much planting should you have?

Obviously the amount of planting depends on the space available. However, a good proportion to aim at is one-third planting to two-thirds open space. The space can be made up of lawn, gravel, paving, water, as well as carpeting plants such as thymes and sedums. In a tiny garden this may sound like too much space and not enough planting, but without the space the full impact of the planting cannot be appreciated.

## How big should beds and borders be?

More often than not, planting areas – beds and borders – are too small to accommodate what is planted in them. Think of an average small shrub, such as *Hebe* 'Red Edge': when mature it could be 90cm (3ft) across and the same high. It will quickly fill and overflow a 60cm (2ft) wide border, and you will regularly be cutting it back to keep it off the grass or path that runs alongside. This means that your low-maintenance shrubby evergreen planting suddenly becomes labour intensive, and looks unattractive as well.

A long, narrow border results in a row of plants and makes it virtually impossible to create interesting planting combinations. It can work if you fill the vertical space above it; this may be possible if the border runs alongside a wall or fence and you plant extravagantly, to create a lush, leafy effect.

For general planting of shrubs, roses and perennials, 1m (3ft) is the absolute minimum width for a border, and it is always better to have one good-sized bed or border than several smaller ones.

Never think that a narrow planting area is easier to maintain than a wider one. With a wider bed you can not only achieve effective ground cover with low shrubs, perennials and underplanting, you can also make best use of bark mulch to control weeds and retain moisture in the soil: if you put bark on a bed less than 60cm (2ft) wide, you will be forever moving it from the adjoining path or lawn back onto the bed. If you are planting trees and shrubs, a wide bed also makes it possible to use a weed-control membrane under the mulch (see page 26–28).

This small garden is beautifully designed and planted, with interest and variety wherever you look. Although the borders are relatively narrow, good use of climbers and slender plants makes the space seem lush and leafy.

# Choosing the plants

**Above:** *Achillea* 'Heidi' makes a dreamy summer combination with *Salvia verticillata* 'Purple Rain' in a sunny border. **Below:** The shell-pink blooms of *Clematis* 'Pagoda' are subtle but strikingly beautiful.

How you put the plants together in your garden determines the overall success of the design. You may be put off by the word design, but any combination of plants is really a design decision; get the combination right and the design works. Ultimately you are looking for a pleasing effect from season to season, with sufficient interest and variety of form and colour. Obviously the starting point is choosing the right plants.

## Plants that work hard

Some plants work much harder than others when it comes to earning their place in the garden. Some of our favourite shrubs, such as syringa (lilac), philadelphus (mock orange) and deutzia, have a relatively short season of interest. Their blooms are glorious while they last, but they quickly fade to leave the shrub as just another mound of matt green in the border. Even repeat-flowering roses have their dull seasons and their cultivation is not always trouble-free. In a large garden there is more scope to include plants that contribute only for a short time, because there is plenty of other planting to take over the show. But in a smaller space it is important to choose plants that earn their keep: plants that look good for most of the year, know their boundaries and need little care and attention.

Your first step should be to select plants with more than one season of interest. Evergreens are the obvious choice, but these are certainly not the only plants that look good throughout the year. You might consider a tree with spring flowers and autumn fruit or leaf colour; beautiful bark could be an added attribute. Shrubs with variegated foliage look good throughout spring and summer; others may have colourful winter stems, as well as attractive summer foliage.

## Judge every plant on its contribution

When choosing, do not think just about flowers; also consider leaves, stems and the plant's shape and texture. More importantly, judge every plant on its merits and what it contributes, rather than on whether you find it individually appealing. Many plants end up struggling in the wrong situation just because the gardener has an aversion to another plant that would truly thrive there. *Aucuba japonica* (the spotted laurel), for example, is great in shade, grows on any soil, is evergreen, has striking foliage and forms a good background for other shrubs; but many gardeners reject it because it is widely planted in commercial situations. The reason it is so often used here is because it is both a survivor and a performer – qualities to draw on for your own garden.

## We all have our favourites

This does not mean you cannot include your favourites, even if their moment of glory is a short one; you just have to take a little care in choosing what you plant them with, or you have to find innovative ways to prolong the season of interest. A later-flowering clematis such as *Clematis* 'Polish Spirit' or *Clematis* 'Prince Charles' can breathe new life into an earlier-flowering shrub such as *Viburnum carlesii* 'Diana' or *Spiraea* 'Arguta'. Alternatively, you could plant a shrub with variegated foliage in that area of planting to liven it up during the quieter summer months.

## One plus one equals three or more

A few clever plant combinations transform a pleasant garden into something special. They may not be associations that last throughout the season, but at the moment when two plants are at peak performance, the effect is far greater than the sum of their two individual contributions. It is easier to achieve this result with foliage plants than it is with flowers.

Dark purple and plum foliage adds depth and drama to any border. The cut-leaved black elder, *Sambucus nigra* 'Eva' (syn. 'Black Lace'), is a wonderfully versatile foliage shrub that mixes well with many other shrubs, perennials and roses. It looks most dramatic when placed with white-variegated or silver foliage. Try it alongside the elegant tall grass *Miscanthus sinensis* 'Variegatus' or the soft silver-grey *Ozothamnus rosmarinifolius* 'Silver Jubilee': both would be stunning combinations of leaf colour, plant form and texture. Also, both combinations would work as a backdrop or centrepiece for the rest of the planting.

Use foliage colour as the canvas on which to paint your flower colours. Lime-green or soft golden leaves make a vibrant backdrop for burgundy or purple blooms. The lovely *Cotinus coggygria* 'Golden Spirit' is at its freshest and most subtle in spring and makes a wonderful partner for deep purple rhododendrons or the lighter purple flowers of *Hesperis matronalis* (sweet rocket) or *Lunaria annua* (honesty). Both of these are biennials, and can easily be introduced by sowing seed directly into the ground alongside the cotinus.

## Buying on impulse

Despite good intentions to plan carefully and select the right plant for the right place, all gardeners buy on impulse. You may declare that you have no further room for plants in your plot, but then you see something you fancy – and you have another little treasure to find room for. This is what gardening is all about, so don't feel guilty!

However, keep the planting picture of your garden in mind, and remember those layers of planting (see page 76). Look out for gaps and consider how new plants can fill them to make the picture complete.

Spring- and summer-flowering bulbs and seasonal bedding plants also come into their own in extending the season of interest. If strategically placed in the border they can take the show over when shrubs and perennials have passed their best. You can also use them to create exciting plant combinations that require little forward planning. See *Annuals and bulbs: Adding extra colour*, pages 128–135.

**Above left**: The shining new leaves of *Cercis canadensis* 'Forest Pansy' are a contrast to the velvety mature foliage that will add depth to any planting scheme. **Below**: *Miscanthus sinensis* 'Variegatus' grown with the black elder *Sambucus nigra* 'Eva' (syn. 'Black Lace').

# Trees *The essentials*

*Acer palmatum* 'Fireglow', a small tree grown here in a pot, brings height, colour and foliage interest to a sunny patio. It makes an engaging partner for the soft plumes of the tender grass *Pennisetum setaceum* 'Rubrum'.

Any garden, however small, needs at least one ornamental tree; the height and vertical interest it contributes make the space three-dimensional and really bring the garden to life. At the same time a tree can have a profound effect on the garden environment. Well positioned, it will provide shade, privacy, a haven for wildlife and a focal point in the landscape. Well chosen, it will provide interest all year round through its silhouette, foliage, blossom and bark.

If you want a tree to have impact from day one, it is probably worth buying time by planting a larger, more mature container-grown specimen.

Trees can be planted bare root or rootballed in late autumn and winter, or as container-grown plants at any time of year. A container-grown tree is a more reliable option because success is almost guaranteed, and you are giving the most important plant or plants in your garden a flying start.

Compared to other garden plants, a tree is a substantial investment. But do not let price determine your decision. After all, this will be a long-term garden feature and, for the years of pleasure that it will bring you, the outlay will be relatively modest.

Do not be put off by descriptions that quote the ultimate size of the tree if this is not

It seems that we are afraid of trees. They grow tall, out of our reach, and beyond our control: a concept that is alien to the gardener used to pruning and trimming and keeping every plant within bounds. How often we hear of trees beheaded in their youth, just because they committed the crime of growing too tall.

Actually it is weight, not height, you should be afraid of. Topping a tree can cause the canopy to thicken and this will have a far greater impact on the garden than allowing the plant to have its head and gain height at will.

The size of tree available to buy depends on speed of growth and variety. When choosing, look more for good shape and branch formation than for size. Avoid any that look as if they have been in their pots for a number of years, waiting to be sold. It is always best to visit a garden centre or nursery and select your tree yourself, rather than buying unseen.

compatible with your timescale. If a description tells you that the tree you would like is going to reach 20m (60ft) in 60 years, ask yourself whether that will concern you. None of us wants to create problems for future generations, but – just like gardeners who have gone before us – we will not necessarily see the results of everything we plant. If you are planting a tree for the future, imagine that, ultimately, you will only be looking at it from above or below, so the most important consideration is what it will do for your garden in the meantime!

## Choosing the right tree for your garden

In a small garden a tree can have a profound effect on the space, extending it vertically and making it three-dimensional. It may be tempting to consider a small weeping or spreading tree because the ultimate height sounds right. However, this type of tree steals ground space and it casts heavy shade beneath its canopy, restricting planting possibilities around it. A tree that provides light airy height, a birch for example, casts only light dappled shade and allows planting right up to its trunk. A slender, compact-headed tree such as *Pyrus calleryana* 'Chanticleer' provides strong vertical structure and will not restrict planting by overshadowing the ground, but do bear in mind that it will not provide a shady place to sit on a sunny day.

The tree or trees in your garden should dominate the uppermost layer of the planting picture. If you choose diminutive and slow-growing trees, and combine them with shrubs that mature more quickly, the trees' scale will be lost and they will be overpowered. It is important to select a tree that will remain in

proportion both with the surrounding planting and with the garden as a whole.

As you consider the options, never lose sight of the fact that a tree, like any other plant, will thrive only if it is happy with the soil, aspect and exposure of the site in which it is planted.

## Do not be bewitched by blossom

Most of us know far less about garden trees than we do about other plants; this isn't surprising since we buy them less often and they need little aftercare. When choosing a tree, think carefully about the contribution it will make to the garden throughout the year, not just about how pretty it looks at the moment you meet it. A young tree bedecked in blossom is hard to resist, but how will it look in autumn – do the leaves colour? How will it look in winter when stripped of its leafy mantle?

*Crataegus laevigata* 'Paul's Scarlet' is a good example of an attractive blossom tree with little else to offer. Often chosen for country gardens, this scarlet hawthorn has a mass of double flowers in May and a loose, informal habit. Yet it can be slow to establish, does not produce any fruit and does not colour significantly in autumn. There are plenty of small flowering trees with much more to offer.

**Left**: The delicate blossom of *Malus* 'Evereste' will be followed in autumn by colourful fruits.
**Below**: A magnolia growing, as so often, beyond its expected size in a small front garden.

When selecting a tree for your garden, never simply follow the lead of your neighbours. In the 1970s this tendency led to vast numbers of stately *Cedrus atlantica* Glauca Group being installed in tiny front gardens, and masses of large-growing magnolias being planted in unsuitable places.

# Trees *If you have only one …*

Perhaps you do not buy, or even look at, trees very often in your life. This is an investment and planting decision that will not only last a long time, but also capture the moment – a bit like giving birth! Here are a few trees that have proved themselves over the years and are sure-fire winners for the smaller garden.

## 1 *Acacia baileyana* 'Purpurea'

This acacia is smaller in stature than *Acacia dealbata*, the florist's mimosa, which grows too large for many gardens. It is one of the most attractive foliage trees, with the bonus of fluffy, scented yellow flowers in spring. The finely divided leaves are bright blue-grey, tinged rich purple at the tips of the branchlets. The tree is light and airy in character and can be lightly pruned after flowering to make a more compact head. Reaching around 4m (13ft) in height in 10 years or so, it is a good choice for a pot. It needs an open sunny position and shelter from cold winds.

## 2 *Acer griseum*

The paper-bark maple is one of the most outstanding small trees – and a good example of one that requires patience. Usually supplied as a small pot-grown specimen, it often grows to only 2m (6ft) in the first 10 years. But do not let this put you off, for it has presence and character from an early age. The peeling cinnamon bark is striking throughout the year and its small leaves cast only light shade. The autumn colour is a rich blend of flame and red. It grows on most soils, although it is not at its best on shallow chalk.

## 3 *Acer palmatum* 'Bloodgood'

One of the more vigorous and upright Japanese maples, growing to 4m (13ft) high in 20 years, 'Bloodgood' has wine-purple, weather-resistant foliage, turning rich red in autumn. It takes some beating as a small, purple-leaved tree and suits most situations, except for cold, exposed sites. Contrary to popular belief Japanese maples do grow on alkaline soils and must have full sun for good foliage colour; they also appreciate shelter from cold winds. They need no pruning or shaping. If you do prune, avoid cutting them in the dormant season as this can result in disease spreading through the branches.

4

5

6

## 4 Betula albosinensis 'Fascination'

A birch is the ideal choice for a small garden: it uses the vertical space and casts only dappled shade with its dainty leaves. This one has dark green leaves, and a more compact head than other birches, but with the same fine filigree of twigs. The bark is copper and cream, sometimes amber and sometimes white, always beautiful. The tree will grow to 8m (26ft) high in 20 years, but its light head means you can grow plants beneath the canopy right up to the stem.

## 5 Cercis canadensis 'Forest Pansy'

This is a lovely alternative to a red-leaved Japanese maple. Its large heart-shaped leaves are velvety purple when mature, shining ruby when young. In autumn they become suffused with gold and flame. The delicate, dark branches can be rather wide-spreading, but this is part of the charm of this gem of a small tree. It grows to around 3m (10ft) in 10 years and, like Japanese maples, is best sheltered from cold winds. It makes a wonderful backdrop to summer-flowering perennials in shades of pastel pink, blue and mauve.

## 6 Cornus 'Porlock'

Perhaps the ultimate small flowering tree, 'Porlock' has elegant horizontal branches carrying semi-evergreen leaves and exquisite creamy-white bracted flowers in late spring. The bracts last for several weeks, blushing pink as they age, and are followed by hanging strawberry-like fruits in autumn. Although exotic in appearance, this cornus is easy to grow on any neutral to acid soil and will tolerate some alkalinity. It will also thrive in a large pot for a number of years if fed regularly with a controlled-release fertilizer. In the open ground it will reach 4m (13ft) in 20 years.

For an important specimen tree, it is worth considering a multi-stemmed birch as an alternative to a single-stemmed standard. To encourage a tree to grow in this way, the main stem is pruned right back, nearly to the ground, in the early stages of growth; this stimulates several stems to grow from just above ground level. They give the effect of an informal group of trees, and you get the benefit of more impact from the line of the stems and the colour and texture of the bark. Both the Himalayan birch (*Betula utilis*) and our native silver birch (*Betula pendula*) are lovely grown in this way.

Small leaves are blessed by the gardener every time they fall in autumn. They rarely cause problems when they descend on grass, beds and borders and are not as likely to block gutters and drains. Sorbus, gleditsia and robinia all have pretty pinnate leaves with small leaflets.

### 7 Crataegus × persimilis 'Prunifolia'

An excellent choice for chalk soils and for cold, exposed sites, this is a compact tree, usually reaching 5m (16ft) in 20 years. Round-headed when young, it spreads more broadly with age. The leaves are rounded and shining emerald green. Clusters of white flowers in spring are followed by large red fruits, which persist on the branches well into winter. In an open sunny situation the autumn foliage colour is truly dazzling, in shades of gold, flame and orange.

### 8 Malus 'Directeur Moerlands'

This is a pretty flowering crab, with red-purple foliage and wine-red flowers in spring. It is an improved form of Malus 'Profusion' and has healthier foliage that resists scab and mildew. It has an open, spreading habit and grows to a height of 5m (16ft) in 20 years. Stunning in spring underplanted with bulbs, it is a useful background tree later in the year; it is not as heavy and dominant as the purple-leaved plum, Prunus cerasifera 'Nigra'.

### 9 Malus 'Evereste'

One of the best flowering and fruiting crabs, this is a small, conical tree with profuse apple-blossom flowers in spring, healthy foliage that turns gold and orange in autumn, and yellow-orange fruits. It grows to 6m (20ft) in 10 years, can be pruned like an apple tree to control its size, and is the ideal choice

11

12

Stake and tie your tree for at least the first three years after planting. Check the ties regularly, and loosen them as necessary as the girth of the stem increases.

Keep newly planted trees well watered during the first year. A length of plastic pipe pushed into the soil, or a plastic water bottle with the bottom cut off and inverted into the soil as a funnel, helps to direct water to the rootball.

Feed with a controlled-release fertilizer in early spring, sprinkling the granules over the soil about 60cm (2ft) away from the main stem.

for anyone who craves apple blossom in the garden but does not like the idea of planting a dreary fruit tree.

### 10 *Prunus maackii* 'Amber Beauty'

This is a tree for the gardener who loves beautiful bark: smooth, silky and light copper in colour, it is seen at its best in low winter sun. The healthy apple-green foliage makes a compact, flame-shaped head, becoming more spreading with age. In spring white fluffy flowerheads grace the branches; in autumn the leaves turn to golden yellow. This wonderful tree grows

to 6m (20ft) or more in 20 years. Plant it to rise from a swirling mass of bronze carex or rich orange-brown *Uncinia rubra*. The cream and pale salmon flowers of *Narcissus* 'Bellsong' are a pleasing spring partner.

### 11 *Pyrus calleryana* 'Chanticleer'

This is widely planted for its compact, flame-shaped head and superb foliage. Growing to around 8m (26ft) after 20 years, it is upright in shape with healthy, shining green leaves that appear early and fall very late, often in December. The foliage colour in autumn is excellent,

often gold suffused with copper and purple. White flowers cover the branches in early spring as the apple-green new leaves unfurl.

### 12 *Sorbus vilmorinii*

Growing to only 3–4m (10–13ft) in 20 years, this sorbus has a slender frame that will fit into the smallest space and is perfect to add height to a mixed planting of shrubs and perennials. It has fine fern-like foliage and small pink fruits that hang in open bunches during autumn and early winter. These follow creamy-white flowers in spring. The leaves turn red and purple in autumn.

# Trees in pots

If you have only a tiny garden, or where you want the effect of a tree without the height, then you can have a token tree, grown in a pot. This could be a trimmed and trained evergreen standing sentinel at the door, or perhaps a gently weeping specimen providing an elegant focal point, whether on the terrace or among other planting. Growing a tree in a pot is a useful way of providing year-round structure in a limited space – and because it is in a container you can move it from place to place and vary the display as you wish.

In large pots most trees will be happy for several years. The container restricts the roots and slows growth as the plant matures. You just have to remember to feed annually with a controlled-release fertilizer, and to be prepared to water regularly. For more information on pots and potting compost, see page 95.

## Naturally dwarf evergreens

Some dwarf conifers are ideal for growing in containers. They have the form of a full-size tree, but are on a much more manageable scale. *Juniperus communis* 'Compressa', for example, has dense, light green foliage and a slender flame-shaped form. Grown in a pot, it will give the effect of an Italian cypress (*Cupressus sempervirens*) in miniature.

## Japanese maples

If you prefer the changing picture of a deciduous tree, a Japanese maple is an obvious choice. The varieties of *Acer palmatum* offer an incredible range of leaf shape, colour and

form, and look effective throughout the year, especially in autumn when the foliage of most varieties intensifies in colour. *Acer palmatum* 'Fireglow', for example, has oxblood-red leaves throughout the summer, intensifying to scarlet in autumn. It will be happy in a large pot for many years. The cut-leaved varieties of *Acer palmatum* 'Dissectum' have dome-shaped heads, and slightly weeping branches as they mature. These are a good choice for those who want weeping trees, which are so much easier to accommodate in pots than they are in the open ground.

## Evergreens for trimming

If you favour a more formal, round-headed tree, there are several evergreens that can be trained as standards and trimmed as neatly as you like.

Left: *Acer palmatum* 'Fireglow' becomes even more colourful in autumn. Below: *Juniperus communis* 'Compressa' will be happy in a pot for many years. Bottom: The olive, *Olea europea*, can be trimmed to make a neat miniature tree.

More vigorous trees put up quite a bit of wind resistance, so do make sure containers are large and heavy enough to prevent them toppling over.

The popular evergreen *Photinia × fraseri* 'Red Robin' is usually thought of as a shrub, but makes a splendid small standard tree if trained accordingly. Trimming results in a flush of new scarlet leaves, so clip it in spring and again in summer. Because it responds well to regular trimming, the ultimate size is controllable. It is an excellent choice for a pot and a cheerful alternative to a standard bay.

*Olea europea*, the olive, is much hardier than many imagine. Rarely seen in gardens a few years ago, olives are now as widespread as eucalyptus, but better behaved. Their silver stems and small dark green, silver-backed leaves are a pleasing contrast to the plain green leaves of many other garden plants.

Beautiful when young or mature, an olive in a pot can be trimmed regularly for more formal effect, or allowed to grow as a loose, airy small standard. As the plant matures the head needs cutting back hard, or pollarding, every few years. An olive is a good choice for a sunny site and, because it tolerates drought, it is ideal if you are likely to leave your garden unwatered for a few days in summer.

## Other evergreens

*Arbutus unedo* 'Atlantic' is a more compact form of the Killarney strawberry tree. A beautiful evergreen with shiny dark green leaves carried on russet stems, it produces attractive pinkish-white flowers and round scarlet fruits, both in autumn. This is a free-flowering and fruiting form and is a good choice for a large pot. Starting life as a shrub, it grows very slowly, but will eventually become a small tree. If you remove the side-shoots from the lower part of the stems, you will reveal the cinnamon-coloured bark and create the effect of a multi-stemmed tree. It does especially well in gardens on or near the coast.

The Portugal laurel, *Prunus lusitanica*, is another excellent choice to train as a small standard tree in a container. Left to grow naturally, it will often form a dense conical shape and this is easily encouraged with occasional pruning. The dark green, shiny leaves have red stalks, adding to the impact. This is a plant you will find ready-trained as a standard, or you may find a smaller specimen offered as a shrub, which you can easily trim into shape by removing some of the lower branches.

The same is true of hollies (*Ilex*). These are usually rather leggy when young so they are easily encouraged to gain height; regular pruning soon develops a head and forms a small standard, ideal for a container.

**Top:** *Arbutus unedo* 'Atlantic' is a superb form of the strawberry tree. **Above:** The glossy, dark green leaves of the Portugal laurel, *Prunus lusitanica,* have attractive red stems. **Left:** *Photinia × fraseri* 'Red Robin' makes an excellent small standard tree for a pot.

Trimmed and trained plants are popular in mainland Europe and you will find all sorts of other evergreens trained as standards that you can use as token trees. These include euonymus, lavenders and rosemaries. These will all require regular pruning to keep them in shape, and in the case of lavender you should sacrifice the flowers to achieve this.

# Shrubs *The essentials*

Shrubs are the backbone of any garden. Whether evergreen or deciduous, they maintain their presence throughout the year, and play a vital role in the middle and lower layers of the planting picture. Most shrubs are easy to grow and require little maintenance – as long as you select the right ones for your situation. Shrubs vary in size from modest, ground-hugging creatures to big, bold characters that will rival the size of most trees. They can provide leaf colour, shape and texture, flowers, winter stems and, most importantly, structure. If you choose wisely, you can create your whole garden using shrubs and maintain colour and interest all through the seasons.

## Pruning

It may seem strange to talk about pruning before anything else, but the first question you ask when you buy a new shrub is always 'When do I prune it?' The poor thing has only just struggled over the edge of the pot and there you are with the secateurs. The most important thing to remember is that you do not have to prune, and the last thing you have to do is to trim all the woody plants in your garden into neat rounded balls – that is unless you are pursuing an interest in topiary.

As far as evergreens are concerned, you prune only to control size and shape, so if you choose the right ones you should have little pruning to do. Deciduous shrubs grown for their foliage may need pruning to tidy them up. They may also need the occasional hard prune to stimulate vigorous growth and superior foliage.

Flowering shrubs are pruned after flowering, cutting out some of the wood that has flowered, allowing new wood to grow from lower down the plant to flower later in the year or the following season. In other words, shrubs that flower in spring are pruned in early summer; shrubs that flower in late summer and autumn are pruned in winter. Of course there are exceptions, but if you remember this as a general rule, you will not go far wrong.

## Buying shrubs

Container-grown shrubs can be planted at any time of year, although aftercare is always easier if you plant in autumn or early spring, when less watering is required. Many shrubs are available in a range of sizes, from those in small 9cm pots to 25-litre specimens that will deliver an instant

When planting, bear in mind that these plants are intended to grow. It is always difficult to envisage the ultimate spread of a newly planted shrub, but do remember that it needs enough space to develop; at the same time, you do not want to leave large gaps of bare soil, which will quickly be colonized by weeds. If you plant too closely, you will devote a lot of time and energy to controlling the plant, and keeping it in its allotted space. This is where choosing the right plant for the situation is so important.

**Left**: The lime-yellow new leaves of *Cotinus coggygria* 'Golden Spirit' make a stunning backdrop for the delicate, soft purple flowers of sweet rocket, *Hesperis matronalis*, in late spring. **Above right**: The young flowerheads of *Hydrangea arborescens* 'Annabelle' open soft green before they turn cream. This is a good shrub for semi-shade and never grows too tall.

When choosing a shrub consider how its position in the garden will influence the overall effect: shape, structure and colour of flowers and foliage all play their part. Yellow foliage attracts the eye, so one golden-leaved shrub will draw attention to that spot. If you use a shrub with yellow leaves on one side of the garden, you probably need to use it on the other as well, to balance the picture.

## Foliage is the most important factor

If you want a long season of interest then foliage should be your first consideration. Some plants flower more than once in a year, and some such as *Viburnum tinus* have long flowering seasons, but the colour and interest provided by leaves lasts for a longer period. This is where evergreen plants have the upper hand; those with colourful leaves can look good for 12 months of the year.

Having said this, deciduous shrubs, like most trees, present a picture that changes with the seasons, and this is a joy in itself: delicate new leaves unfurling in spring, the heavy mantle of summer, and glorious autumn colour. In an ideal world you will have a well-chosen mixture of evergreen and deciduous subjects that will provide colour, texture and interest throughout the year.

**Above:** *Itea virginica* 'Henry's Garnet', an outstanding plant for long-lasting autumn colour. **Below:** *Cornus mas* 'Variegata' is one of the finest deciduous variegated shrubs.

effect in your garden. Obviously the price increases with size. The majority of gardeners will go for two- or three-litre plants, with one or two larger specimens in key positions where immediate impact is desired.

## Choosing shrubs

Often we choose a plant we are familiar with, one we like when we see it in flower or berry, but we give little thought to what it looks like for the rest of the year. As with all plants, some shrubs work harder than others in making their contribution to the garden. These are the ones to look for, particularly if you are gardening in a small space. You want as long a season of interest as possible for the minimum amount of effort. A well-chosen shrub will deliver this more efficiently than any other plant.

# Small shrubs  *If you have only one ...*

If you have space for only one or two small shrubs – in other words those that normally grow to no more than 1m (3ft) in height and spread – evergreens are an obvious choice, especially those with attractively coloured or variegated foliage. However, there are also some deciduous shrubs that give a long season of interest and produce flowers as an added bonus.

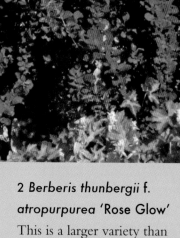

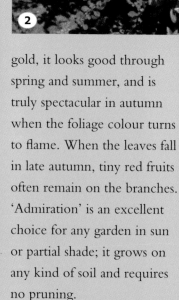

It is always difficult to estimate the ultimate size a plant will reach; it depends upon the soil and conditions in which it is growing. Some of the plants on these pages will eventually grow to more than 1m (3ft) in height; those that do will respond to occasional pruning and can be easily controlled.

**1 *Berberis thunbergii* f. *atropurpurea* 'Admiration'**
A striking, compact shrub, this berberis is suitable for the smallest garden as it grows to only 45cm (18in) high and the same across. With rounded habit and red-purple leaves delicately edged with gold, it looks good through spring and summer, and is truly spectacular in autumn when the foliage colour turns to flame. When the leaves fall in late autumn, tiny red fruits often remain on the branches. 'Admiration' is an excellent choice for any garden in sun or partial shade; it grows on any kind of soil and requires no pruning.

**2 *Berberis thunbergii* f. *atropurpurea* 'Rose Glow'**
This is a larger variety than 'Admiration', usually growing to 1m (3ft) high and across. The leaves of the young shoots are purple, heavily marked with salmon pink. The variegation is lost as the leaves mature; those further down the stems eventually turn to a deeper purple. The

shrub has an open, graceful habit and colours richly in autumn. Tiny red berries persist on the branches after the leaves have fallen. There are other similar varieties, including *Berberis thunbergii* f. *atropurpurea* 'Harlequin'. All are easy to grow and require little or no attention.

### 3 Convolvulus cneorum

This low, rounded shrub is ideal for well-drained soil in a sunny situation; it is a good choice for a pot or for a paved or gravel area and is particularly useful in coastal gardens. The silky silver leaves look good throughout the year and the pure white trumpet flowers, flushed salmon on the outside, are produced throughout summer. Rarely growing to more than 60cm (2ft) in height and spread, the plant requires little attention to keep it in shape. Older specimens can be lightly pruned in spring to promote new growth.

### 4 Euonymus fortunei 'Silver Queen'

Perhaps the best variety of this familiar evergreen, 'Silver Queen' forms a spreading shrub up to 90cm (3ft) high and a little more across, but it grows slowly. The sage and dark green leaves are boldly edged and variegated with creamy white, and are sometimes almost entirely white. This heavy variegation is responsible for its slow growth rate. It thrives on any soil, in sun or shade; it will also make a good short evergreen climber if grown against a wall. It is an excellent choice to lighten the shade under a tree.

### 5 Hebe 'Red Edge'

This ever-popular hebe forms a dense mound of upright stems crowded with grey-green leaves that flush purple-red at the tips in winter. It does not open up in the centre of the bush like many hebes; instead it retains its neat dome shape for many years; nor does it ever suffer from the leaf spot diseases that trouble some of these useful shrubs. It grows slowly to 90cm (3ft) high, with a similar spread. Small panicles of white flowers appear in summer, acting as a magnet to bees and butterflies.

### 6 Osmanthus heterophyllus 'Goshiki'

Often mistaken for a dwarf holly, this osmanthus forms a dense, rounded shrub with shining spiny leaves of dark green, heavily mottled and patterned in cream and bronze. When grown in full sun the colour is usually lighter and more yellow. The young foliage near the branch tips is light copper in colour, making the plant a striking focal point in any border throughout the year. It needs no pruning, and there are no obvious flowers, so no dead-heading is required. Happy on any soil, 'Goshiki' grows slowly to 1m (3ft) in height and spread in 10 years or more, and looks good from an early age.

### 7 Photinia × fraseri 'Little Red Robin'

This is a new, dwarf form of our most popular evergreen shrub. The stems are upright in habit, with shiny, gently waved, dark green leaves. The new growth, produced at any time of the year, is bright scarlet. The shrub grows to around 1m (3ft) in height and spread and can be trimmed to control size and to encourage a new flush of red shoots. Despite its recent introduction, 'Little Red Robin' is already a favourite for small gardens and pots.

### 8 Pittosporum tenuifolium 'Tom Thumb'

This is a wonderful dwarf evergreen shrub, growing slowly to a dome 1m (3ft) high and across. The leaves are chocolate-purple, shining and gently waved, on finely branched stems. In spring the new growth emerges as soft peridot-green shoots all over the bush, making a striking contrast to the dark mature leaves. As the days shorten in late autumn, the foliage becomes darker and more intense, turning shining purple-black as winter progresses. The foliage is particularly beautiful when etched with frost or lit by a low winter sun. This shrub makes a wonderful planting partner for silver-variegated shrubs, winter heathers or early spring bulbs such as snowdrops.

### 9 Sarcococca confusa

Christmas box is a versatile evergreen shrub forming a clump of upright green stems carrying dark emerald shining leaves. It grows to about 80cm (32in) in height and spreads slowly to 1m (3ft) across. In late winter, tiny pinkish-white tufted flowers appear in the leaf axils. Although not showy to look at, they are deliciously scented and will fill the whole garden with their fragrance. Glossy black berries often follow the flowers and persist until the following winter. This is a superb shrub for any soil in sun or shade, and particularly useful under trees. It is also good for cutting for the house.

## 10 Skimmia × confusa 'Kew Green'

Unlike many skimmias, 'Kew Green' tolerates sun, and the foliage does not go yellow and chlorotic. It forms a dome-shaped evergreen shrub up to 80cm (32in) high and about 1m (3ft) across, with rosettes of emerald-green leaves carried on green stems. In autumn large clusters of green flower buds appear; these open to yellow-green, richly fragrant flowers in early spring. This skimmia does not produce berries but it makes up for this with its excellent flowers and foliage. Skimmias grow on any fertile soil, as long as it is well drained, but are not at their best on shallow chalk.

## 11 Spiraea japonica 'Firelight'

This is a hard-working deciduous shrub with soft golden, red-tinged foliage throughout the spring, summer and autumn. It is at its loveliest in spring when the new growth emerges flame orange. As the leaves develop, the colour becomes more yellow, but with red highlights at the branch tips. The deep pink fluffy flowers are of secondary importance to the leaves. In a sunny site, autumn colour is good; when the leaves fall they reveal a mass of fine, light tan stems that have surprisingly strong colour in the winter light. With a low, rounded habit, this spiraea grows to 90cm (3ft) high and across, but can be trimmed annually in late winter to maintain a more compact shape and remove the faded flowerheads.

Those with acid soil could choose any of the dwarf rhododendrons or evergreen azaleas. For example, the early-flowering Rhododendron 'Patty Bee' is a fine dwarf variety with rounded dark green leaves that tint bronze in winter. Pretty, pale yellow flowers appear in early spring. It is also worth considering heathers. Many ericas, such as Erica × darleyensis 'Darley Dale', flower in winter, providing welcome colour when other shrubs are sleeping. Some callunas, such as Calluna vulgaris 'Firefly', have colourful foliage as well as summer flowers.

## 12 Viburnum davidii

Widely planted because it succeeds in any situation on any soil, *Viburnum davidii* is nonetheless a magnificent plant, with great foliage and a compact, domed habit. The leaves are dark green, leathery and deeply veined and carried on red leaf-stalks. The clusters of tiny grey-white flowers are insignificant, but on female plants they develop into metallic blue-black berries. If you want a plant that berries, buy it when it is in fruit; it is the only way to tell male from female. The shrub can reach 1m (3ft) in height and spread, but is usually smaller than this. It can be pruned, makes an excellent low hedge and is brilliant in a pot.

# Small shrubs for pots

Small shrubs, especially evergreens, make excellent permanent subjects for pots; if you have a patio, courtyard or balcony, this is undoubtedly how you will grow them. The containers you choose, how you group them together, and how you position them will have a dramatic effect on the appearance of your garden throughout the year.

Most of the plants described in the preceding pages would do well in pots; here are a few more small shrubs that are particularly successful. These can, of course, be grown in the open ground, if you have the right soil.

### 1 Buxus sempervirens 'Elegantissima'

This elegant variegated box has small leaves of dark green edged with cream, giving a light and delicate effect. In a pot it grows slowly, to 60cm (2ft) high and across in 10 years; it responds well to clipping, and makes a good long-term container plant. Unlike the plain-leaved species, it rarely suffers from nutrient deficiency, which shows as bronzing of the foliage. It grows well in sun or shade and is very frost-resistant.

### 2 Itea virginica 'Henry's Garnet'

This is a small deciduous shrub growing to 80cm (32in) high, with a spread of 60cm (2ft). In spring, long oval apple-green leaves unfurl and long fluffy heads of creamy-white flowers appear. In autumn the leaves turn garnet red and last on the branches well into winter; when they finally do fall, they reveal cinnamon-coloured twigs. Grow this lime-hating itea in John Innes lime-free compost, and give it a sunny position for the best autumn colour.

### 3 Leucothoe 'Lovita'

This is a lovely evergreen, with dark green foliage that turns deep claret red in winter. Dwarf and compact, it forms a spreading shrub that reaches only 30cm (12in) in height and spread. It does well in sun or shade, but the winter foliage colour is stronger in a sunny position. It hates lime, so should be grown in John Innes lime-free compost.

### 4 Phormium 'Alison Blackman'

Phormiums are really evergreen herbaceous perennials, but they have become honorary shrubs in our gardens. Their spiky leaves provide a welcome contrast to the soft, rounded shapes of most shrubs, and they make dramatic and interesting plants for large, deep pots. 'Alison Blackman' is a most attractive variety with short, broad, upright leaves of olive green, boldly edged and striped with rich cream, with a delicate deep orange margin. It will grow to 1m (3ft) high, with a similar spread. All phormiums with colourful leaves dislike poor drainage and still, cold conditions. They do best in full sun, but will tolerate

Growing in pots enables you to overcome soil conditions – you are in control. This is the way for those gardening on chalk to grow lime-hating subjects.

a little shade. In containers give them a good depth of compost and make sure it is free-draining.

### 5 *Phormium cookianum subsp. hookeri* 'Cream Delight'

This phormium has dark emerald leaves, gracefully dropping at the tips, with a broad cream band in the centre and finer cream stripes at the edges. It is similar in stature to *Phormium* 'Alison Blackman' and needs the same growing conditions.

### 6 *Pieris japonica* 'Katsura'

Pieris are superb ericaceous shrubs with fine foliage, colourful new growth, and beautiful flowers resembling lily-of-the-valley. 'Katsura' is a relatively new variety, fairly compact and growing to 1m (3ft) in height and spread, with glossy dark green leaves, and deep mahogany new leaves arranged in rosettes at the branch tips. The flowers, borne in spring, are deep soft pink carried in delicate sprays that lie gracefully across the upper leaves. This is an outstanding plant for a patio container in semi-shade and

For shrubs in pots use John Innes No.3 compost, or John Innes lime-free (ericaceous) compost for lime-hating plants such as rhododendrons and azaleas. Choose large, well-proportioned containers; avoid ones that narrow at the neck as these make re-potting difficult. Leave a generous gap of 3cm (1in) between the top of the compost and the rim of the pot, to allow for watering. Scrape away the surface of the compost each spring, add a generous handful of controlled-release fertilizer, and top up with fresh compost.

will be happy for many years in a pot of lime-free John Innes compost.

### 7 *Pieris japonica* 'Little Heath'

This is another wonderful pieris, with small sage-green leaves edged with soft creamy white. Growing to about 80cm (32in) high and the same across, it is compact and bushy with copper-coloured new growth, and bears small white flowers in spring. Although it is not particularly free-flowering, this is one of the finest dwarf shrubs for foliage. It likes the same growing conditions as *Pieris japonica* 'Katsura'.

### 8 Rhododendron (Azalea) 'Johanna'

Evergreen azaleas have declined in popularity in recent years, perhaps because we overdosed on them in our gardens previously. Some are poor subjects that shed much of their foliage in winter to leave bony stems supporting a gaudy display of flowers in spring. If this is the image you carry of an evergreen azalea, look again. Some are excellent foliage plants with year-round appeal, and they are exotic flowering shrubs at the same time. They lend themselves to pots and

containers, especially those with a light glaze and an oriental look. *Rhododendron* 'Johanna' is one of the finest, with upward-sweeping stems carrying rich green shining leaves that tint copper-red in winter. The late spring flowers are deep red and look stunning against the leaves. This is a fairly compact shrub, growing to 60cm (2ft) high with a spread of 80cm (32in). Plant it in a pot of lime-free John Innes compost, ideally in a lightly shaded spot.

See also *Pots and containers*, pages 136–137.

# Larger shrubs  *If you have only one …*

Larger shrubs, grown primarily for their foliage, are the framework of a good garden. These serve as the backdrop for the detail planting and hold the scheme together. As they occupy the layer of the planting picture at eye level, they are a particularly important part of the view from the windows of the house, so they need to provide interest for much of the year.

### 1 *Cornus alba* 'Sibirica Variegata'

This dogwood has dark red stems in winter, and green leaves boldly edged and variegated with cream and pink throughout summer, changing to pink and burgundy in autumn. Some cornus are rather too large for a small garden, but this one will fit in anywhere as it grows only 1.2m (4ft) high and the same across. It will thrive on any soil, in sun or shade, and needs little attention, apart from occasional hard pruning if you want the best stem colour. In that case, cut the stems back to 10cm (4in) above the ground in March every couple of years; this promotes vigorous upright growth, good foliage and brighter winter bark colour. Unpruned, it develops a more branched, twiggy habit.

### 2 *Cornus mas* 'Variegata'

A slow-growing deciduous shrub, this cornus has pointed oval leaves, dark green with broad creamy-white margins, carried on slender, straight twigs. In late winter, tiny fluffy yellow flowers are produced on the bare stems. These are followed by small red, cherry-like fruits in autumn, which make a lovely contrast to the variegated leaves before they fall. This is a refined shrub that takes time to mature, but it is well worth waiting for. It can reach 1.5m (5ft) in height and spread and will grow on any soil, in sun or shade.

### 3 *Cotinus coggygria* 'Golden Spirit'

This is an unusual variety of smoke bush with rounded leaves of golden yellow with a hint of lime. The foliage is more lime green when grown

**4**

**6**

in shade, and also early in the year when the leaves unfurl. The autumn colour is brilliant flame orange before the leaves fall. 'Golden Spirit' is upright in habit, usually slow-growing when young, then more vigorous, reaching 2m (6ft) in height with a spread of 1.2m (4ft). It is happy in any soil. Cotinus respond well to hard pruning in late winter and this stimulates strong growth and good foliage.

### 4 Euonymus japonicus 'Chollipo'

This is a fine form of this versatile evergreen, which grows on chalk or clay, in sun or shade, on dry soil or in salt winds. 'Chollipo' is dense and upright in habit, eventually reaching 2m (6ft) in height and 1.2m (4ft) across, but is easily controlled at virtually any size by trimming. The

leaves are deep emerald green broadly edged with bright yellow. It is an excellent choice as a screening plant. It also grows well against a wall or fence, and would make a perfect partner for a yellow-leaved shrub such as *Lonicera nitida* 'Baggesen's Gold'.

### 5 Griselinia littoralis 'Variegata'

This is another good choice for an evergreen with gold-variegated leaves. If it has a limitation, it is that it dislikes chalk and alkaline clay soils. It grows particularly well by the coast, in sun or shade, and its yellow-variegated olive-green leaves and yellow-green stems are a welcome contrast to the heavier, darker green of many evergreen shrubs. It is upright and bushy and will reach 3m (10ft) high, with a spread of 1.5m (5ft) or more, if allowed

to. It responds well to clipping and makes a lovely hedge. Cut out any plain green shoots if they appear.

### 6 Phillyrea angustifolia

A member of the olive family, *Phillyrea angustifolia* has small narrow, emerald evergreen leaves carried on upwardly sweeping stems. It forms a compact and rounded bush, eventually reaching 2m (6ft) in height and spread. Although not immediately striking as a young plant, it is a good choice since there are few light, feathery evergreens – most are heavier in character. It makes a good screening shrub, responds well to pruning, and is wonderful to cut for flower arranging. It is easy to grow in sun or shade on any well-drained soil and is a superb coastal plant.

Not all taller shrubs are greedy for space. Some are comparatively slender and can be accommodated in a smaller garden, especially those like pittosporum and euonymus that respond well to light pruning to keep them under control.

**5**

### 7 *Physocarpus opulifolius* 'Diablo d'Or'

Dark burgundy-wine leaves tinged copper at the tips are the strongest feature of 'Diablo d'Or'. The clusters of small pinkish flowers in early summer are of secondary importance, but they are often followed by copper-red seedheads. This is an upright shrub, growing to 1.2m (4ft) high and the same across. Although it loses its leaves in winter, it has bright tan-orange stems that are attractive in their own right. It is a brighter and bushier form of the popular *Physocarpus opulifolius* 'Diabolo' and is a better choice for a smaller garden. It grows on any soil in sun or partial shade.

### 8 *Pittosporum tenuifolium* 'Elizabeth'

This light, airy shrub has small, rounded oval leaves of soft sage green variegated with white and delicately edged with pink, more so in winter. It is bushy and upright in habit, and more compact than the popular *Pittosporum* 'Garnettii'. It responds well to clipping and is excellent for cutting for the house. Left to grow naturally it reaches around 2m (6ft) in height, with a spread of 1.2m (4ft). For smaller gardens choose *Pittosporum tenuifolium* 'Irene Paterson', which is smaller, growing slowly to 1.2m (4ft) high and 1m (3ft) across; it has pale green leaves heavily suffused with white, and often almost entirely white at the tips of the branches. Both varieties grow on any well-drained soil, in sun or shade.

### 9 *Pittosporum tobira* 'Variegatum'

This pittosporum has interesting whorls of narrow leaves, which are broader near the stem tips. The colour of the foliage is soft sage green, marbled with darker green and tipped and edged with cream. It forms a rounded shrub up to 1.2m (4ft) in height and spread and is a good choice for a sunny sheltered garden or one near the coast. The flowers are creamy, fading to yellow, and are produced at the branch tips in late spring; they are delightfully fragrant. Both

Larger shrubs can be grown in large pots and containers. These are useful near the house where there is no soil to plant them in the ground. A large shrub in a pot can also serve as a screen to hide the wheelie bin, water butt, gas bottles or any other eyesore.

**10**

**11**

**12**

If you want to control the size of an evergreen shrub, start to prune it lightly and regularly while it is within reach and within your control. If in doubt, prune evergreens in early spring, just before the next flush of growth is about to appear. If you prune when the plant is small, you should be able to do this with secateurs, thus avoiding the half-cut leaves and untidy effect that result from using shears.

this and the plain green-leaved species respond well to pruning and are very drought-tolerant.

## 10 *Rosmarinus officinalis* 'Miss Jessopp's Upright'

Of all rosemaries, this is one of the best. A most attractive and versatile shrub, it has upright stems that add vertical interest to any planting scheme, and narrow, silver-tinted dark green leaves on grey stems that fit in anywhere. The pale blue flowers early in the year are an added bonus and a welcome companion for spring-flowering bulbs; the aromatic foliage is nice to touch and enjoy, both in the garden and in the kitchen. Left unpruned it

grows to 1.2m (4ft) in height and spread, but it is easily controlled by cutting back some of the older stems by half to two-thirds in spring, straight after flowering. Rosemary will grow on any soil but prefers poor, well-drained soil in full sun.

## 11 *Sambucus nigra* 'Eva'

More often known as 'Black Lace', this is the finest of the ornamental elders. Although the plant is deciduous, it makes up for its lack of leaves in winter with spectacular summer foliage, and large flattened heads of pinkish flowers. The leaves are finely divided and shining, rich dark purple. They are a superb addition to any mixed planting scheme, and

a marvellous partner for any other colour. Not as vigorous as some elders, 'Eva' grows to 1.5m (5ft) high and the same across. It needs light pruning, or can be cut back hard in February; hard pruning results in vigorous growth and larger leaves and is the best treatment for young plants. It thrives on any soil and the foliage colour is strongest in full sun.

## 12 *Viburnum tinus* 'Eve Price'

This viburnum is hard to classify as it is both an excellent flowering shrub and a wonderful foliage plant. It delivers everything you ask for in a shrub: easy to grow, compact in habit, evergreen, and in bud and flower for

half the year. It is therefore not surprising that this plant is so widely used in gardens and commercially; do not let that put you off. *Viburnum tinus* grows under trees, on clay and chalk, and does well in containers. 'Eve Price' has smaller leaves than many other varieties, and a dense bushy habit. It grows slowly to 1.5m (5ft) in height and spread and produces abundant clusters of pink buds in autumn, which open to white flowers in late winter and early spring.

# Flowering shrubs *If you have only one ...*

If you are going to plant a flowering shrub in your garden, then you want one that is a reliable performer, and one that looks good throughout the rest of the year, when it is not in bloom. We are fortunate that we have such an amazing range to choose from, and we all have our favourites. Here is a collection of superstars that are sure to put on a wonderful display year after year.

### 1 Camellia × williamsii 'Jury's Yellow'

This is a fine variety of the 'queen of shrubs'. Upright in habit, it is slow-growing and compact, possibly reaching 90cm (3ft) in height in five years, with a spread of 60cm (2ft). The foliage is glossy dark green and as much a reason to grow a camellia as the flamboyant blooms. 'Jury's Yellow' has creamy-yellow anemone-form flowers. These have large petals on the outside and smaller ones in the middle. They are produced in late winter and early spring and fall from the plant as they fade. This is the major advantage of the *Camellia × williamsii* varieties, because the overall effect is not ruined by faded flowers. Camellias need neutral to acid soil. Those gardening on alkaline soils can grow them in pots o lime-free John Innes compos Avoid an east-facing situation as the early morning sun can spoil frosted flowers.

### 2 Ceanothus 'Concha'

This ceanothus may flower only once, in late spring, but its sapphire display is hard to resist. It is perhaps the best evergreen ceanothus, forming an arching shrub up to 2m (6ft) in height, with a spread of 1.5m (5ft). The leaves are small, shining and rich green. The flower buds are reddish before the fluffy blue flowers open and smother the branches, usually completely concealing the leaves. Because of its upright habit it is ideal against a wall or fence. Ceanothus like full sun and well-drained soil. They are not long-lived plants, usually surviving for about ten years, but they grow quickly initially, so are a good choice for the impatient gardener. The evergreen ceanothus dislike pruning. For a small garden, you may prefer the deciduous

*Ceanothus* × *delileanus* 'Gloire de Versailles': although it is not as spectacular, it has a long flowering season, lasting right through summer and autumn. This shrub can be cut back in February to control its size and shape.

### 3 *Ceratostigma willmottianum*

The hardy plumbago is a superb low-growing shrub that comes into its own later in the year. It starts to bloom in late summer, and as autumn progresses the delicate foliage takes on reddish hues and the rich blue flowers are produced in even greater profusion. This is such an easy plant to care for on a well-drained and sunny site: cut it back hard in early spring to promote vigorous growth and a bushy habit. It can grow up to 1m (3ft) in height and spread, but is usually much shorter.

### 4 *Choisya* × *dewitteana* 'Aztec Pearl'

This is one of the most beautiful evergreen flowering shrubs. The narrow leaflets give the plant a lightness absent from many evergreens.

Pink buds open to fragrant white flowers with golden stamens. These are carried in large clusters all over the shrub, in spring and again in autumn. Rounded and bushy in habit, it grows slowly to 1.5m (5ft) in height, with a spread of 1.2m (4ft), and succeeds in sun or light shade on any well-drained soil. Choisyas can be slow to grow for the first year after planting; if you are not prepared to wait, you should invest in a larger specimen.

### 5 *Cistus* × *obtusifolius* 'Thrive'

One of the hardiest, most durable varieties of cistus, 'Thrive' forms a dome-shaped shrub, up to 90cm (3ft) in height and spread, and unlike most cistus will tolerate light

clipping to create a more formal effect. The growth habit is dense and bushy and the leaves small and dark green. Shining white, yellow-eyed flowers smother the shrub in early summer and sprinkle it intermittently throughout the rest of summer into autumn. This is an excellent drought-tolerant plant for a sunny position and is great for coastal gardens.

### 6 *Cistus* × *pulverulentus* 'Sunset'

This is a low-growing mound of a shrub usually no more than 60cm (2ft) high, with a spread of 90cm (3ft). The felted soft green leaves look good throughout the year. If cistus have one drawback it is the limited extent of their colour palette: the flowers are either white or a shade of pink. 'Sunset' is one of

**7**

**9**

**8**

the most vibrant, with bright purple-pink, yellow-eyed flowers. It is a good choice to plant alongside silver foliage plants or perhaps a purple sage. It loves full sun and grows on any well-drained soil; it is at its best on chalk or growing through gravel.

### 7 *Daphne bholua* 'Jacqueline Postill'

Perhaps the finest hardy plant for fragrance, this daphne will fill the whole garden with its sweet perfume. It makes a somewhat upright shrub, up to 1.5m (5ft) high and 1.2m (4ft) across, with flexible tan-coloured stems and emerald evergreen leaves. The foliage is sparser on poor soils and in cold conditions. The flower clusters open in late winter from purplish-pink buds to creamy-pink flowers, richly scented and profuse, and a mature shrub in full flower is a marvellous sight. It is at home in either sun or semi-shade, and on most soils; although often recommended for acid soils, it grows successfully on chalky soils of reasonable depth. It does not grow well in a pot.

### 8 *Escallonia* 'Apple Blossom'

This is a compact variety of this popular evergreen.

Small, leathery dark green leaves on green twigs make a well-branched shrub that sits happily alongside perennials, roses and deciduous shrubs. It is free-flowering, producing a mass of pink and white flowers in summer. 'Apple Blossom' grows slowly to around 1m (3ft) in height and spread and can be pruned to reduce its ultimate size. Escallonias are drought-tolerant, good by the coast and will put up with chalk; they prefer a sunny situation.

### 9 *Grevillea* 'Rondeau'

This Australian native is fairly new to our gardens and has proved surprisingly hardy in a sunny situation on well-drained soil. Growing to about 1m (3ft) in height, with a spread of 1.5m (5ft), it has an open, spreading habit, straight stems and narrow olive-green leaves, often tinged bronze at the tips of the shoots. A relative of the protea, it has interesting crimson honeysuckle-like flowers in clusters, all along the branches and for a very long period. Plants often start to flower as early as February and continue until July. It is ruined by trimming. If you need to prune at all, cut back some of the longest shoots in midsummer, as soon as flowering has finished.

### 10 *Hydrangea serrata* 'Bluebird'

This hydrangea is a dainty character with purple-tinged leaves and lacecap blooms that are pinkish lilac on chalk, and gentian blue on acid soils.

These turn red–purple with hanging florets in autumn; they are wonderful to cut for the house with a few late roses. 'Bluebird' makes a compact and upright shrub, growing to 1m (3ft) high and the same across. Happy in sun and lovely in light shade, it will grow on any well-drained fertile soil. Trim off the old flowerheads and any dead stem tips in February, cutting back to the first pairs of fat buds behind last year's flowers. On mature plants a few of the older stems can be cut back to ground level.

The mention of hydrangeas conjures images of big, bold blooms of deep pink, blue and white outside seaside cottages, or perhaps decorating the stage at a summer event. Reliable shrubs, the mophead and lacecap hydrangeas were widely planted during the mid-1900s, but have been considered rather old-fashioned in recent years. However, there are many fine varieties – for flowers, stems and foliage. *Hydrangea macrophylla* 'Preziosa' has dense heads of deep pink flowers, turning claret in autumn, and purple-tinged leaves. *Hydrangea* 'Zorro' is a magnificent new variety with black stems.

10

## 11 *Potentilla fruticosa* 'Primrose Beauty'

Although potentillas are not at their best in winter, when they appear as a tangled mass of brown stems, they come into leaf early, start to bloom soon afterwards, and carry on flowering well into autumn. Few other garden plants put on such a performance. 'Primrose Beauty' is one of the best varieties of this popular shrub, with pretty grey–green, finely divided leaves and pale primrose buttercup-like flowers. It grows up to 90cm (3ft) in height and spread and is best lightly trimmed in winter to remove old flowerheads and keep the plant in shape. It will grow in either sun or light shade on any well-drained soil, including chalk.

## 12 *Weigela* 'Kosteriana Variegata'

Pleasingly variegated foliage adds to the attraction of this summer-flowering shrub. The leaves are broad, green in the centre and generously margined with creamy yellow. In autumn they become tinged with pink and orange-red, remaining on the plant for several weeks before falling. In early summer, the pink funnel-shaped flowers combine attractively with the leaves. A compact shrub of rounded shape, it grows to about 1m (3ft) high and the same across. It is happy on any soil, in either sun or light shade. Cut back some of the branches that have flowered as soon as the blooms fade, to encourage new vigorous growth.

11

12

# Roses  *The essentials*

Roses may be the nation's favourite flowers, but they are by no means the easiest of plants to grow. Yes, their blooms are wonderful, sumptuous and sensuous, with character and fragrance. But roses need pruning, they need feeding, they are prone to disease, and they are probably as far away from being low-maintenance plants as anything in the garden. Yet none of this puts us off persevering with them, whatever the time in our gardening life.

## Selecting varieties

There are certainly more varieties of rose to of plants. New ones are constantly being introduced, with better disease-resistance, flower power and growth habit. So there is no point whatsoever in hanging on to a sickly rose that demands constant attention, always looks unhealthy, and fails to perform. The best thing to do is to get rid of it and plant a good one.

In small gardens it is important to consider the length of the flowering period, and how much space a rose plant occupies. Some of the old-fashioned shrub roses can be large and may flower for only a brief time. Some climbers and many ramblers are just too rampant, and you may curse the amount of waste they generate when you come to prune them, if you have the energy to climb a ladder to reach them.

## What type of rose should you choose?

Many roses sell because of their name. Occasion roses, celebrating an event, an anniversary or a birthday, are popular gifts but are not necessarily the best choice for your garden when you are looking for performance. If someone buys you one of these, think carefully how you use it. A pot may be the best place for it until you decide whether it is worth planting permanently.

David Austin's compact English roses are wonderful plants with beautifully formed flowers and delightful fragrances; they also flower repeatedly throughout the summer and beyond. These are a good choice, especially the newer varieties. Many can be grown as short climbers: these are ideal for smaller gardens and require less maintenance than more vigorous climbers and ramblers.

Varieties of *Rosa rugosa* are excellent on sandy, light soils and near the coast. These are disease-free and need little pruning; they can get rather big, but their fragrant blooms and showy hips make them well worth growing where space allows. They make a superb security barrier and are usually left alone by deer and rabbits.

Some of the smaller old-fashioned shrub roses are worth considering, particularly those

**Left**: The rugosa rose *Rosa* 'Fru Dagmar Hastrup' is a good choice on light, sandy soils and is relatively disease-free. The single blooms are fragrant and produced freely.
**Below**: *Rosa* 'Sweet Dream' is a delightful, compact patio rose, great for pots or narrow borders.

that flower more than once in the season and offer good resistance to disease.

Patio roses, smaller-growing floribundas, are good for pots and in small gardens. Some, such as *Rosa* 'Sweet Dream' with peachy orange flowers and glossy green foliage, have established themselves as favourites in the past few years. Others are only seen for sale when in flower in early summer, alongside the bedding plant selection in garden centres. They provide a colourful display, but most lack fragrance.

Patio climbers are semi-climbing varieties of patio rose. These are an excellent choice for small gardens, growing in pots on balconies and wherever a manageable climber is required.

## Growing conditions

Roses like heavier soils and, unlike most gardeners, they adore clay. Clay provides the stability and the water- and nutrient-holding capacity that these plants require. They like plenty of organic matter added to the soil, ideally in the form of well-rotted farmyard manure. They also need an open position, without too much competition from neighbouring plants, if they are to perform at their best.

Some roses will grow in semi-shade; generally varieties with yellow blooms are the best choice here. Some will grow on light, sandy soils, and most do well near the coast, where the good air movement helps to prevent disease.

The large, fragrant blooms of the English rose *Rosa* 'Jubilee Celebration' are carried gracefully on arching branches. It sits well with perennials such as nepeta, geranium, sedum and penstemon.

Despite the narrow border, this garden wall is transformed with extravagant drapes of *Rosa* 'Teasing Georgia' and the gloriously fragrant *Rosa* 'Snow Goose'.

## Planting roses

Roses can be planted as bare-root stock in autumn and winter, and into early spring. Container-grown stock is widely available and can be planted at any time of year. The containerized plants offered for sale during autumn and winter have been potted only recently and, as roses have rather a bony root system, the compost often falls away from the roots when you take the plant out of its pot. This is not a problem if you plant the rose firmly, to the same depth as it was in the pot.

Contrary to popular belief, you can plant a rose where another has died, or has been removed. The old course of action was to dig a large hole, remove the soil and replace it with fresh soil from another area of the garden. This is no longer necessary if you use Rootgrow, a preparation of beneficial mycorrhizal fungi. This comes in a granular form and is sprinkled at the bottom of the planting hole. The fungi soon colonize the rose's roots, supplying extra water and nutrients to the plant, which helps it to establish quickly and enhances growth and flowering.

## Feeding

Roses are hungry plants that need plenty of nitrogen for leaf and stem growth, and plenty of potash for flower production. They also need magnesium, iron and trace elements to be successful. We expect a lot from our roses in terms of flowers so it is important to keep the nutrients they require readily available. Also remember that strong growth is more disease-resistant; weak-growing roses are the ones likely to fall foul of disease. A generous application of a quality rose fertilizer should be made in early spring, as the plants start to grow, and again in midsummer, after the first main flush of flowers has faded. Sprinkle the fertilizer around the plants, work it into the surface of the soil with a hoe, and water thoroughly.

## Watering

Roses need moisture: dry conditions around the roots can lead to mildew on the foliage. Mulch your roses in summer with good garden compost or well-rotted stable manure and water regularly in dry spells, keeping the water off the flowers and foliage. A soaker hose laid across the soil surface, and covered with a thick layer of bark, is an effective way to water without wasteful run-off.

## Pruning

Traditionally roses were tidied up in autumn and pruned in early spring. Today pruning should be done in midwinter, soon after Christmas. This is because roses start into growth earlier. If they have already produced a lot of new growth, and you cut this off when you prune them, you will put extra demands on the plants by forcing them to make new growth all over again. If you prune early, the subsequent new growth will be tougher because it grows slowly and should be more resistant to disease.

Hybrid tea and floribunda roses are hard pruned, cutting back the stems to three or four buds above ground level. Today we grow more English roses, which are pruned more lightly to encourage bushy, twiggy growth, and more flowers at about 1m (3ft) above ground level. Remember that hard pruning results in vigorous growth, while light pruning results in lighter, branched growth.

Most rambling roses flower only once, in midsummer: after their blooms have fallen, cut back some of the stems that have flowered to encourage fresh, strong shoots to grow from the base of the older stems. Most ramblers are too vigorous, untidy and high maintenance for smaller gardens.

Climbing roses are often climbing sports of bush roses and are pruned lightly to encourage flowering. Training the shoots horizontally helps them to produce side-shoots and more flowers. If the wall or fence is fitted with horizontal wires before planting, this makes training easier.

Patio roses and patio climbers require only light pruning to tidy them and remove any dead and diseased wood.

## Dead-heading

Dead-heading your roses is an excellent way to keep your plants in trim. Rather than removing individual flowers just below the head, remove the whole truss when petals start to fall from most of the flowers. Cut back to two or three leaves behind the flowerhead. This promotes strong shoots that will flower later in the season.

## Controlling disease

The first steps in successful disease control are: choose disease-resistant varieties, feed them regularly and grow them well.

You do not have to spray your roses as long as you are prepared to put up with a little blackspot and mildew on occasions. Vigilance reaps rewards: if – or rather when – either of these does appear, you should pick off any infected foliage as soon as you notice it.

If you are going to spray, start early and spray at regular intervals according to the manufacturer's instructions. It is a good idea to vary the product you use to prevent the disease becoming resistant to a particular chemical. Spray the foliage thoroughly, moistening both surfaces of the leaves. You do not need to use a combined pest and disease spray if there are no insect pests such as greenfly on your plants; just use a fungicide on its own.

English roses, herbaceous perennials and alliums paint a colourful picture in this summer border. Underplanting with dwarf narcissi and other spring-flowering bulbs would add interest at the beginning of the year.

Pot-grown roses can be successfully planted in midsummer when in flower. Choosing them at this time of year enables you to see exactly what the flower looks like, and you can smell it – scent is a rose's most important attribute.

# Roses  *If you have only one ...*

If you have space for only one rose in your garden, choose from those featured here. These roses are selected for their garden performance, for their resistance to disease and to weather, and for the quality of their flowers. They are mostly English roses, but one or two others that have outstanding qualities are also included.

**1 *Rosa* 'Cornelia'**

This is a hybrid musk rose, an old-fashioned rose that repeat flowers, with loose clusters of strawberry-pink blooms tinged with gold. The scent is strong and delicious. Growing to something over 1m (3ft) in height and spread, it makes a loose shrub with reddish stems and dark green foliage. It is excellent for a larger bed, or in a mixed border of shrubs and perennials.

**2 *Rosa* 'Crocus Rose'**

Although it is not widely planted, 'Crocus Rose' is considered to be one of the best of the English roses. Strong-growing and free-flowering, it reaches over 1m (3ft) in height, and a little under in spread. The large, rosette-shaped apricot-cream flowers become fuller and paler with age; they are freely produced in clusters at the end of arching stems.

**3 *Rosa gallica* var. *officinalis***

Known as the 'apothecary's rose', this is the oldest rose in cultivation. Although it normally flowers only once in midsummer, it makes up for this by producing plenty of blooms that open in succession. The semi-double flowers are crimson, opening wide to display their golden stamens, and have a strong old rose fragrance. The foliage is light green, healthy and very resistant to disease. This rose will grow to about 1m (3ft) in height and spread. It is a survivor, doing well even on poor soil, and it mixes well with other plants. It is the ideal choice for gardeners who 'don't do' roses.

## 4 Rosa gallica 'Versicolor'

Formerly known as *Rosa mundi*, this famous old rose has all the qualities of *Rosa gallica* var. *officinalis*, but its blooms are crimson striped with white, rather like raspberry-ripple ice cream.

## 5 Rosa 'Jude the Obscure'

This English rose is the perfect choice for those looking for an old-style rose. Exceptionally large, incurved blooms of softly shaded yellow are carried with good foliage on bushy plants, growing to about 1m (3ft) in height and slightly more in spread. The fragrance is the main attribute of this rose: strong, fruity and reminiscent of sweet dessert wine. There are few gardeners who are not captivated by its charms. It is a magnificent rose and does particularly well in a warm, sunny situation.

## 6 Rosa 'Lady Emma Hamilton'

From the time this English rose comes into leaf, you know it is going to be good. The dark green leaves are strong and healthy and are enhanced by copper new shoots. The flowers are globe shaped, red in bud opening to soft glowing apricot-orange, with a rich, fruity fragrance. Reaching about 1m (3ft) in height and spread, it remains healthy throughout the season, as long as it is not crowded by its neighbours.

## 7 Rosa odorata 'Mutabilis'

A total contrast to the large, opulent double-flowered varieties, this China rose is a graceful creature with slender growth and delicate single flowers. The blooms open soft creamy yellow, change to copper-orange and then to soft crimson-pink. All colours are represented in a flower cluster at the same time, and the blooms are produced with remarkable continuity. The leaves are narrow, dark green and flushed with dark red. This is a tall, light rose that can reach 2m (6ft) in height and a little less in spread, but is easily contained to a more compact size. It is a good choice against a sunny wall and an excellent alternative to a climber.

## 8 Rosa 'Princess Alexandra of Kent'

This English rose is a recent introduction, and set to be an enduring favourite. With very healthy growth, it forms a compact shrub up to 1m (3ft) high and across. The large cupped, upward-facing

fruit-scented. This is a very different colour for a shrub rose, and a good choice to plant alongside yellow-variegated or golden foliage, where pink or red roses would look out of place.

## 11 Rosa 'The Mayflower'

This has to be one of the easiest roses to grow. It forms a strong twiggy bush, less than 1m (3ft) in height and spread, with matt green foliage that remains disease-free throughout the season. The flowers are double, deep pink and fragrant and are produced all summer long. 'The Mayflower' is another of the English roses and a great choice for a small garden and for poor soil.

## 12 Rosa 'Young Lycidas'

See this new English rose in bloom and you will be unable to resist it. Its glorious pointed buds open into full opulent blooms of magenta-purple. The wonderful perfume is everything you would expect from such an exquisite flower. The foliage is healthy and emerald green, and the shrub grows to about 1m (3ft) in height and spread.

blooms are beautifully poised, and of rich glowing pink, paler towards the outside. The scent is a fresh tea fragrance, becoming lemony as the flower ages.

The following taller-growing English roses make excellent short climbers; all are fragrant and repeat-flowering:
'A Shropshire Lad' (peachy pink)
'Snow Goose' (white)
'Teasing Georgia' (deep yellow)
'The Pilgrim' (yellow)

## 9 Rosa 'Rhapsody in Blue'

This is a modern shrub or floribunda rose with semi-double blooms of soft purple-blue that fade to grey-purple as they age; they have a strong orange fragrance. The unusual colour and free-flowering habit make this a superb rose to plant with other shrubs and perennials, particularly those with grey foliage. It is a tall rose, growing to 1.2m (4ft) with

a spread of 1m (3ft), so is better planted further back in a border.

## 10 Rosa 'Summer Song'

An upright rose, reaching about 1m (3ft) high and a little less in spread, this English rose can be pruned to grow taller or shorter, according to the situation. The lovely open cup-shaped flowers are deep burnt orange in colour, and are heavily

# Growing roses in pots

Roses can be successfully grown in pots as long as you remember their requirements. Choose a pot that is at least 40cm (16in) across, and similar in depth. A traditional flowerpot shape is ideal because this has a large surface area of compost for watering and feeding. Fill the pot with John Innes No.3, a loam-based potting compost that will support the plant physically, as well as holding on to the water and nutrients your rose requires. As when planting in the open ground, plant the rose at the same depth as it is growing in the container in which you buy it.

Add a generous handful of rose food to the compost when you plant your rose and do the same each spring and midsummer, just as you would for roses in the open ground. Alternatively, you can use a controlled-release fertilizer, and water during the summer months with tomato fertilizer to supplement the potash. This may fit in better with your container-maintenance regime if most of your plants are in pots and you are also growing a few tomatoes.

Roses in pots require regular watering during the summer months, but they will cope with a few days of neglect if you are away for the weekend. Each spring, scrape off the top 2–3cm (¾–1in) of compost and replenish with fresh John Innes. This helps with the nutrient content, and should remove any disease spores that are hanging around on the soil surface.

## Good varieties for pots

Any of the patio roses, compact floribundas, are suitable for growing in pots; so are some of the smaller English roses and these will give the large flowers that most gardeners expect. The varieties featured here are particularly good in containers, but equally excellent in the open ground.

### 1 Rosa 'Darcey Bussell'
This is a fine English rose that flowers freely throughout the summer, producing clusters of beautifully formed, many-petalled blooms of deep crimson. It is a compact and bushy plant, less than 90cm (3ft) in height and spread.

### 2 Rosa 'Grace'
This English rose has rosette-shaped apricot flowers and light apple-green foliage. The growth is light but well branched and the fragrant flowers are produced repeatedly throughout the summer. The blooms are weather-resistant and the foliage remains healthy. What more could you ask for? 'Grace' can grow to about 1m (3ft) in height and spread, but is usually rather smaller than this in a pot.

### 3 Rosa 'Jubilee Celebration'
Free-flowering and deliciously fruit-scented, this English rose has opulent, rounded blooms of rich salmon pink with golden highlights on the underside of the petals. The flowers are held above the foliage and well displayed, despite the fact that the stems arch under their weight. It can grow to around 1m (3ft) in height and spread, but is easily contained.

### 4 Rosa 'Queen of Sweden'
Upright and bushy, growing to about 1m (3ft) high and 60cm (2ft) across, this is an English rose that takes up little space, but rewards with healthy dark green foliage and delightful cup-shaped blooms of pure soft pink. The flowers are lightly scented, freely produced and wonderfully weather-resistant.

# Climbers  *The essentials*

Climbers are versatile plants that can bring walls and fences to life, soften pergolas and arches, and extend the season of trees and shrubs over which they scramble. Some also make good ground-cover plants. Climbers can quickly bring maturity to a new garden, and in established planting are a welcome addition, one for which you can always find space. In the smaller garden climbers are particularly useful in borders too narrow for larger shrubs; here they can create a luxuriant effect and add valuable height.

Most climbers require some attention. By nature a climbing plant needs a support of some form or other, and many need pruning to remove old stems and restrict potential size. A climber may also need training to encourage it to grow where you want it to, rather than where it naturally wants to scramble.

## How climbers grow

It is worth considering how and why climbers grow in the way they do before you select them. Some produce aerial roots that are able to cling onto relatively smooth surfaces such as bare walls and fences. These root-clingers, such as ivies and climbing hydrangea, are the most self-sufficient climbers; they may need guiding towards their support initially, but once they get a good grip they largely fend for themselves.

Other climbers, including wisteria and honeysuckle, have twining stems that they wrap around supports such as posts or poles or the stems of other plants. Some, such as passion flower, produce tendrils, which they coil round a support, while others – like clematis – use twining leaf-stalks. All of these appreciate a little help to start climbing: when you plant them, tie their stems up with soft twine or stretchy plastic ties. After this, tying in should be needed only to direct the growth where you want it to go.

Plants such as climbing roses haul themselves up by using their thorns as hooks; others simply scramble, pushing their long lax stems through neighbouring plants and over nearby objects. Both types will need new growth tying in place throughout the season, otherwise they will become a mass of tangled stems.

**Left**: The cerise, white-eyed flowers of the rambling rose *Rosa* 'American Pillar' are bold and beautiful against the wine-red foliage of the flowering crab apple *Malus* 'Directeur Moerlands'.

*Clematis armandii*, the evergreen clematis with large leaves, is a strong grower, valuable for its foliage and early white or pink flowers. It can look very tatty if grown in an exposed position and may require a lot of maintenance to restrict its size and remove old stems and leaves.

All ivies tend to be tarred by the same brush; they are seen as aggressive characters that wreck brickwork, invade the ground and kill trees. This is untrue, but it often prevents them being used in situations where they would simply be the best choice. On shady walls they provide year-round interest and colour – and they require little attention.

Often a climber is seen struggling against a wall, with only the prospect of scrambling up a piece of trellis usually far too small to support it. On walls and fences the most suitable method of support is strong galvanized or plastic-coated wire stretched between screw-in vine eyes. The climber can then be tied to the wires to encourage it to climb in the right direction.

**Above**: The deep purple-green foliage of *Hedera helix* 'Atropurpurea'. **Right**: The ruby-flowered *Clematis* 'Abundance' and the satin-purple *Clematis* 'Royal Velours' forge a pleasing partnership.

## Some good climbers for low walls

*Clematis alpina* varieties

*Clematis macropetala* varieties

*Euonymus fortunei* varieties

× *Fatshedera lizei*

*Hedera helix* 'Glacier'

*Hedera helix* 'Goldchild'

## Some good evergreen climbers

*Clematis cirrhosa*

*Euonymus fortunei* varieties

× *Fatshedera lizei*

*Hedera colchica* varieties

*Hedera helix* varieties

*Jasminum polyanthum* (for warm sheltered gardens)

*Schizophragma hydrangeoides*

*Trachelospermum jasminoides*

## Types of climbing plant

Some climbing plants are herbaceous. They die back to ground level at the end of the growing season and start again the following year from the roots, or from seed if they are annuals. These plants sound easy to manage in the garden; you simply clean up the old stems during winter. There are drawbacks, however. Some are rampant and may be too vigorous for you. For example, *Humulus lupulus* 'Aureus', the golden hop, throws up many scrambling stems, which can reach up to 5m (16ft) long. On the other hand, the annual sweet pea (*Lathyrus odoratus*) is shorter in stature, but the plant dies early in the season once it has achieved its objective: to flower and set seed for the coming year. Either you take the time to find another plant to replace it, or you have to put up with an unsatisfactory gap in the planting for the rest of the season.

Other climbers produce woody growth. Their stems remain from year to year, even if they drop their leaves in winter. They have the ability to keep on growing, so may require pruning to restrict their size and spread.

Most deciduous climbers are nothing but a tangle of bare stems in winter. In a small garden this can be unattractive, so you need to position them carefully. Alternatively, choose an evergreen climber – although unfortunately there are relatively few on offer.

## Choosing the right climber

Although garden centres and nurseries sell vast numbers of climbers every year, the true potential of these plants is rarely realized, usually because the wrong one is chosen in

the first place. How often a vigorous, upright climber is chosen for the wall of a bungalow or a low fence: the result is bare stems with a few leaves and flowers at the top. The secret of success is to think of a climber as any other plant: before you buy it, take into account its habit, its potential size and its suitability for the situation you have in mind.

The same applies when it comes to colour, whether of flowers or foliage, and to flowering time. Do not think of the climber in isolation, but in terms of how it will fit into the broader picture. If chosen well, climbers can create an exciting colour combination with a companion tree or shrub, or a second flowering season. They can also be planted together: two climbers growing as one have more impact, and they take the variety show of a border skywards.

# Climbers *If you have only one ...*

All gardens have space for at least one climber – most have room for several. These are valuable plants that provide a lot of interest, but need little input from you.

### 1 *Actinidia pilosula*

This is a striking climber that deserves wider use. Vigorous twining stems carry long, pointed dark green leaves on red leaf-stalks. The end third of each leaf is white on the surface, just as if it has been dipped in paint. In early summer, small pink delicate flowers hang from the branches. Although it loses its leaves in winter, its twining stems are not unattractive. Happy in sun or part shade on any well-drained soil, it grows to 4m (13ft) high; you can prune it in winter if you want to control its size. Because of its tough constitution it is a good choice for a large pot and will cope with some lack of water.

### 2 *Clematis cirrhosa* var. *purpurascens* 'Freckles'

This is a lovely form of the fern-leaved clematis. The pretty, finely divided dark green leaves are glossy on the upper surface, and they tinge bronze in winter. The hanging bell-shaped flowers are basically cream, but are so heavily spotted and blotched maroon on the inside that they appear deep pink. They are lightly lemon-scented and start to open in autumn, continuing into winter. *Clematis cirrhosa* is a native of the Mediterranean so prefers a sunny sheltered position, where it will grow to 3m (10ft) or more. Prune lightly after flowering to control size and shape; if it gets out of hand, you can cut it back hard after flowering every few years. It will succeed on any well-drained soil and will happily grow through a large deciduous shrub or up a small tree, clinging on tenaciously with its twining leaf-stalks.

### 3 *Clematis* 'Fuji-musume'

One of the finest large-flowered clematis, 'Fuji-musume' blooms twice, once in early summer and again in autumn. The flowers are perfectly formed, upward-facing and 12cm (5in) across, in a delightful shade of sky blue with soft yellow stamens. The plant is compact in habit and, using its twining leaf-stalks, climbs to a height of up to 2–3m (6–10ft). Prune in winter, cutting back each stem to a plump pair of buds; if stems are cut to various heights then the plant will remain furnished

Climbers can be successfully grown in pots to provide interest on walls and fences where they cannot be planted in the ground; this is often the case with the walls of the house. Alternatively, they can be grown on short obelisks, which are ideal by the front door or on the patio. Put crocks or stones, for drainage, in the bottom of a large, deep pot at least 40cm (16in) in diameter and fill with John Innes No.3 compost. If the support for the climber is going in the pot, put it in at the time of planting. Add a handful of controlled-release fertilizer at planting time and annually thereafter.

with flowers and foliage from top to bottom. It is a good choice of climber to grow in a pot; although it likes a sunny position, its roots are best shaded by mulching the compost surface with gravel.

### 4 Clematis 'Prince Charles'

This is a superb late-flowering clematis, with the excellent *Clematis viticella* in its parentage. This means that it can be cut back to around 60cm (2ft) from the ground in late winter – a simple way of pruning. It is easy to grow, in sun or partial shade, and is very resistant to clematis wilt. The flowers are profusely produced on the current season's growth, in late summer and early autumn. With blooms of light blue with a hint of mauve, this climber is a wonderful mixer, and will look good with any other colour. It has light, well-branched stems, and reaches around 4m (13ft) in height, by means of twining leaf-stalks. Clematis grow on any soil but they prefer ground with plenty of organic matter and a fair amount of moisture. They struggle to establish on dry, sandy soils.

### 5 Hedera colchica 'Dentata Variegata'

Of all the large-leaved ivies, this is perhaps the finest for the small garden. Its leaves are dark green and sage in the centre, broadly margined and marbled with rich cream. The effect is showy but subtle and works well on its own, or as a backdrop for other planting. This root-clinging climber will grow on any soil, in any situation. It is a natural choice for a shady wall where it will add colour and interest throughout the year. Because of the strong variegation in the leaves, it grows more slowly than many others, eventually reaching a height of 3–4m (10–13ft). It is easily kept in check by light pruning at any time of the year. The foliage is healthy and weather-resistant.

### 6 Lonicera similis var. delavayi

This is a disease-resistant evergreen honeysuckle, less prone to mildew and less rampant than the popular *Lonicera japonica* 'Halliana'. It has fairly stiff twining shoots, with dark green, oval pointed leaves. The flowers are creamy white, ageing to yellow, and are produced in clusters in the leaf axils towards the end of the shoots in late summer. They are sweetly fragrant, as you would expect from a honeysuckle, and a welcome addition to the garden late in

(7)

(8)

(9)

have to replant annually. It is a wonderful subject for a pot, or planted where it can be allowed to scramble over low shrubs. The 2m (6ft) stems are very slender and twining, with small heart-shaped, dark green leaves. The flowers are produced very freely throughout summer and autumn. Each has a bell-shaped outer skirt of red-purple and an inner tube, flared at the end, of purple-black; the effect is exotic and striking. This plant is easy to grow in any sunny situation and can be raised from seed sown indoors in early spring.

## 8 Rosa 'The Pilgrim'

This is an English rose suitable for growing as a tall bush or a short climber. The habit is tidy, and the foliage emerald green and disease-resistant. The deliciously scented blooms are shallow cups, filled with many layers of petals, warm yellow in the centre and paler on the edge of the flowers. They are freely produced throughout summer and into autumn. Grown against a wall or fence, or up a pole or obelisk, it will reach 2.5m (8ft), and

it succeeds in sun or partial shade. Tie in the stems with flexible plastic tie in winter. Like all roses it needs a good, fertile soil and twice-yearly feeding with a rose fertilizer (see pages 105–106). Other than this, light pruning in midwinter and regular dead-heading is all the maintenance required. If pruned lightly from an early age it should produce flowers and foliage from head to toe, unlike many climbing roses, which become bare at the base as they get older. 'The Pilgrim' is lovely planted with a pale blue clematis, such as 'Prince Charles' (see page 115).

## 9 Rosa 'Warm Welcome'

This miniature climbing rose is suitable for the smallest of spaces as it grows only to around 2m (6ft). The flowers are pretty and open in shape, and a wonderful glowing shade of orange. It flowers continuously from early summer into autumn, and will perform on any fertile soil in sun or partial shade. The growth is neat, bushy and upright and the foliage emerald green and healthy. This is a rose that will remain

the season. The plant grows to 4m (13ft) or so and can be pruned in winter to restrict its size. Honeysuckles grow on any type of soil, in sun or shade, and twine happily through trellis, over garden buildings, and into trees.

## 7 Rhodochiton atrosanguineus

This is a tender perennial normally grown as an annual, although it may survive from year to year in a very sheltered location. It is well worth growing even if you

clothed in flowers and foliage from bottom to top. Besides regular feeding, it requires only dead-heading in summer and light pruning in winter. It looks lovely grown up a stout stake or obelisk as a pillar rose, to rise from lower planting. Tie in the stems with flexible plastic tie.

### 10 Solanum laxum 'Album'

This is a strong-growing, scrambling climber with slender stems and leaves, often reddish purple later in the year. Light, open heads of yellow-eyed, white-petalled, potato-like flowers are freely produced from late spring into early winter. It will grow up to 6m (20ft), but can be cut back to the main stems in winter every two or three years. Its light, airy habit and long flowering period make it a good choice to grow with climbing roses or clematis with a shorter season. It will grow on any well-drained soil, in sun or partial shade.

### 11 Trachelospermum jasminoides

This has all the qualities you will look for in a climber. Upwardly mobile twining stems carry small leathery, dark green shiny leaves. The foliage is evergreen and turns a lovely shade of burgundy-red in winter when grown in a sunny position. The fragrant, white jasmine-like flowers are freely produced over a long period during summer. Trachelospermum is not too vigorous, and grows neatly to 3–4m (10–13ft) in height. It succeeds on any well-drained soil in sun or partial shade. Cut back unruly stems at any time of year. The dark green foliage and creamy-white flowers work well as a background for white tulips in spring and white lilies in summer.

### 12 Wisteria brachybotrys 'Shiro-kapitan'

Short panicles of large fragrant, pure white flowers are the hallmark of this lovely wisteria. These unfurl with the new leaves in late spring; usually a second smaller crop of blooms appears in late summer. The young shoots are silky, and the leaves soft green. All wisterias are strong-growing and vigorous twining climbers, but can be controlled to less than 4m (13ft) in height by regular pruning in summer and winter, when the growth is slender and light. The shoots are shortened in late summer, to 30cm (12in) from the main stem. In midwinter these shortened shoots are pruned back to five or six buds; this builds up the spurs that produce the flowers. Wisterias grow on any well-drained soil, in a sunny site or a partially shaded one. Plant with a viticella clematis, such as *Clematis* 'Purpurea Plena Elegans', to provide further interest in the latter part of the year. The clematis can be cut back to 40–60cm (16–24in) above the ground in late winter.

# Perennials  *The essentials*

*Helianthus* 'Lemon Queen' is a wonderful perennial sunflower that lights up the back of the border in autumn. Here its sunny blooms are complemented by the rich golden leaves of *Rhus typhina* 'Tiger Eyes'.

Some repetition in a planting scheme pays dividends. If you have space, try using different sized groups of the same plant in the same border: for example, a group of three achilleas in one position, then a single plant further along amid a drift of geranium. This helps to tie the whole planting together, balances the colour spread, and stops the effect becoming too busy. Remember too that restricting the plant palette makes maintenance easier: you do more of the same thing at the same time.

Perennials have enduring appeal. Most are easy to grow, and because their height is finite we know what to expect from them. The popular garden varieties clump up quickly and soon fill gaps in the border. It is always so satisfying to see that small pot with a couple of shoots that you buy in spring manage to put on such a show later the same summer.

Perennials do have their disadvantages. Most are deciduous herbaceous plants and so they die down to ground level in winter, leaving you to clean up the remains. Many need support of some description: either sticks or grow-through metal supports that have to be put in place before the plants need them. Some of the more vigorous varieties need lifting and dividing every two or three years, to prevent overcrowding in the border and to stop them taking over. Some of our favourites, such as oriental poppies and bearded irises, bloom early and then die back, leaving gaps in the border.

There are, however, plenty of perennials to choose from; if you select self-supporting types that flower for a long period and require only occasional division, they are as near to low-maintenance plants as you can get. Herbaceous geraniums, phlox, asters, rudbeckias and heleniums are just a few popular perennials that deliver a lot for little input. Some grow so easily that they sprinkle seedlings through the border. The random appearance of self-sown plants such as *Verbena bonariensis*, *Digitalis lutea*, *Linaria purpurea* and *Aquilegia vulgaris* can create a soft naturalistic effect and provide the repetition that gardens often lack. Take care to weed out a few seedlings each year before they get out of hand.

Some perennials make excellent ground cover, filling the space under roses and shrubs, and suppressing those annual weeds that could take advantage of bare ground. *Symphytum caucasicum* does an excellent job under shrubs in shade and rewards with sapphire flowers in spring. *Alchemilla mollis* grows anywhere and makes a soft green carpet with a foam of lime-green flowers through summer. These are great plants for that problem area of the garden.

Some perennials have fantastic foliage and will add season-long colour and interest to borders and patio containers: hostas spring to mind, as do heucheras, which these days are every bit as popular. The bold architectural foliage of plants like rodgersia and euphorbia is a useful contrast to the softer, lighter form of ferns and grasses.

## A great way to add colour

Perennials are the ideal way to add colour to your garden and they enable you to experiment with colour combinations. Buying container-grown plants in bud or flower may not be the most economical way to acquire them, but it does allow you to try them alongside other plants and so discover the most successful partnerships before you actually put the plants in the ground.

You can use perennials in front of, or alongside, earlier-flowering shrubs to prolong the season of interest. Summer-flowering perennials are often planted with roses to fill the gap after the first flush of flowers, before later blooms appear. Many perennials combine beautifully with grasses to create a prairie effect; the bold blooms of echinaceas, rudbeckias and heleniums work well in this situation.

## Planting quantities

Most books advise planting perennials in threes or fives. This is fine if your bed or border is large enough to accommodate a bold clump, or if you are planting small specimens early in the season, rather than larger pot-grown plants later on. In a smaller space use your discretion. Use groups of three small plants of things that grow quickly and where you want a drift rather than an exclamation mark. For example, *Nepeta* × *faassenii* would make an impressive drift in the first season. *Penstemon* 'Andenken an Friedrich Hahn' should only be planted as a single specimen, unless you are gardening on estate proportions: plant a group of three in a small garden in spring and you will have to move out by July.

There are more new varieties of herbaceous perennials than there are of trees and shrubs, because perennials are simpler to propagate, and the timescale involved is much shorter. The technique of micropropagation has revolutionized perennial production, making it possible to produce thousands of plants from a single individual in a short time. This also means that perennials are relatively inexpensive to buy.

**Above left:** The beautiful blooms of *Iris ensata* may be short-lived but the sword-shaped leaves contribute to the planting throughout spring, summer and into autumn. **Above:** The flower spikes of *Dierama dracomontanum* have a delicate transparency: wonderful for foreground planting. **Below:** Hostas and grasses add sophistication with colour, texture and contrast.

# Perennials *If you have only one ...*

There are many flowering perennials to choose from, so selection is difficult. Those featured here are easy-to-grow, reliable performers that will fit into virtually any garden. All are chosen because they need minimal attention, and all are self-supporting in ideal growing conditions. With taller subjects on exposed sites, and if in doubt, put grow-through supports or twigs in position when the plants are only a few centimetres high.

### 1 *Achillea 'Terracotta'*

This is a popular and widely available variety of this useful group of perennials. The fern-like foliage is soft sage green, and forms a loose clump of shoots in the border. From mid- to late summer, 40–50cm (16–20in) high stems carry flattened heads of soft terracotta flowers, which age to yellow-ochre. Achilleas prefer a sunny position, and this one needs it for richly coloured blooms. In a lightly shaded site, or sometimes in a dull season, the flowers will open yellow and remain that colour until they fade. As the flower stems are shorter than on many other varieties, 'Terracotta' needs little support. It grows on any well-drained soil that does not become too dry in summer and it does particularly well on chalk. The flower colour makes a lovely combination with any blue plants in the border, such as nepeta, salvias or herbaceous geraniums.

### 2 *Aconitum 'Spark's Variety'*

A tall, late-blooming perennial, this is an easy-to-grow alternative to the ever-popular delphinium. With the potential to reach 1.2m (4ft) in height, its strong stems carry finely divided dark green leaves and branched spikes of inky blue flowers in late summer. Many other varieties of aconitum have denser, heavier flower spikes which, although showy, can look clumsy in the garden. It grows on any soil, and it prefers partial shade. It is slow to clump up (so rarely requires division) and is not greedy of ground space, making it suitable for smaller gardens and narrow borders. It is ideal for growing behind lower plants and is a superb planting partner for roses and early-blooming perennials and shrubs. The plant is poisonous if eaten so is left unharmed by rabbits, deer, slugs and snails – unlike delphiniums, which seem to be relished by pests of all shapes and sizes.

### 3 *Alstroemeria 'Cahors'*

One of a number of good new varieties of the Peruvian lily, this is more compact than many of the older forms, with stout fleshy stems, around 60cm (2ft) high, carrying long-lasting, exotic flowers.

These are salmon with brushstrokes of rose-pink, and each one has three golden yellow petals speckled with deep brown. Blooms start to appear in early summer and continue right through autumn; they are excellent for cutting for the house. Alstroemerias grow from fleshy tuberous roots and are surprisingly hardy, requiring no winter protection in milder areas. They like a sunny situation and well-drained soil. The compact hybrids require no support.

## 4 Aster novi-belgii 'Sapphire'

This is one of the finest and most free-blooming Michaelmas daisies. Dark green leaves clothe well-branched stems, 80cm (32in) high, and these are topped by a mass of rich blue, golden-eyed daisy flowers in late summer and early autumn. The blooms are long-lasting and weather-resistant, and the strong stems need little or no support, despite the weight of the flowers. Michaelmas daisies are renowned for their susceptibility to mildew. 'Sapphire' is one of the

exceptions, with healthy foliage that remains deep green rather than turning grey and powdery. It is easy to grow on any soil in an open sunny position. It looks lovely alongside any deciduous shrub or tree that colours well in autumn; try it with *Berberis thunbergii* f. *atropurpurea* 'Rose Glow'.

## 5 Astrantia major 'Gill Richardson'

With its deep red blooms and dark stems, this is a gorgeous variety of astrantia. The flowers are around 2cm (¾in) across, and the bracts that surround them are tipped with burgundy-black, making them even more striking in the border. The flower stems emerge from a mound of shining, deeply

cut leaves, any time from early summer onwards. They grow to a height of 30cm (12in) and need no support. If you cut them back after the first flush of flowers, new leaves and flowers will appear for a repeat performance. Astrantias grow on any reasonably moist, fertile soil in sun or partial shade.

## 6 Digitalis lutea

A modest little perennial foxglove, *Digitalis lutea* forms clumps of dark green foliage that last for several seasons. The flower spikes are upright, slender and gracefully curved at the tips, usually reaching around 50cm (20in) in height. The tubular flowers are soft greenish yellow – a subtle shade to mix with any other

plant, whether grown for flowers or foliage. It blooms from early summer and is wonderful when allowed to drift through planting, where it will provide that light, spiky height that is so valuable in the garden. The plant readily self-seeds, but is easily controlled, and you will welcome its random appearance because of its ability to fit in anywhere. It grows in sun or shade on virtually any soil.

### 7 Geranium 'Jolly Bee'

This is one of the longest-blooming and most reliable herbaceous geraniums. Forming a large mound of marbled foliage, around 30cm (12in) high and up to 90cm (3ft) across, it is an excellent ground-cover plant for sun or partial shade, and for any well-drained soil; it does particularly well on chalk. The lovely saucer-shaped blue

flowers have conspicuous white eyes and black stamens, and are produced throughout summer and into autumn, until the first frosts. This is a drought-tolerant geranium that also looks attractive in a large pot or container, where it will flow gracefully over the edges. The name 'Jolly Bee' was inspired by the honey bees that flock to the delightfully scented flowers in search of nectar.

### 8 Helleborus × hybridus

The Lenten rose is an essential in any garden. The leathery dark green leaves, popular for their architectural quality, are carried on stout 30–45cm (12–18in) stems and form vigorous clumps. They are best removed in late autumn to allow the flower stems freedom to rise from the ground, ready for the delicate, saucer-shaped flowers to open in late winter. Hellebore flowers come in a wide variety of soft and sophisticated colours, both simple and intricately patterned. Plants are easy to grow, but they prefer neutral to alkaline soils and do not like extremely wet or dry

conditions. They do well in dappled shade, so are ideal set between deciduous shrubs and other perennials, where they will add winter colour and interest. Named colour selections are available, but to avoid disappointment be sure to buy plants that are in flower, so that you can see for yourself what the blooms look like.

### 9 Nepeta × faassenii

Soft blue flowers and grey-green leaves make catmint a particularly good mixer and a useful softener of paving, walls and steps. The flowers are produced continuously from early summer into autumn. It grows to about 30cm (12in) high, with small leaves and a light, flowing habit. The stems do flop over if not supported, but this encourages new stems to emerge from the centre of the plant. For a tidier clump, position a grow-through support over the plant in early spring, or cut back the outer stems halfway through the growing season. Nepeta grows on any soil, and does particularly well on chalk. It loves hot dry, sunny situations, making it a natural partner for silver foliage subjects, which also thrive in such conditions.

## 10 Penstemon 'Raven'

Penstemons bridge the gap between herbaceous perennials and shrubs in that they have woody stems that do not die down in winter; they are also evergreen. There are many varieties to choose from, ranging from small alpines to large, spreading border beauties. 'Raven' is slender and upright in habit, so easier to accommodate in the smaller garden. The stems reach 80cm (32in) or so, and are topped by spikes of large tubular flowers of the deepest purple, from early summer right through to autumn. Penstemons should be dead-headed as the flowers fade, tidied up in autumn and cut back by half to a third in spring. If you cut them back right to the base, they will not start to flower until autumn. They are drought-tolerant plants that suit sunny situations. They last for several years on well-drained soil, but are shorter-lived on damp sites and heavy clay.

## 11 Pulmonaria 'Lewis Palmer'

This is one of the finest lungworts for early flowers and beautiful foliage. A clump-forming perennial growing to 20cm (8in) high, it will fit into the smallest garden. It revels in shade or partial shade, and it will grow on any soil, but dislikes dry conditions; it does particularly well on heavy clay and in moist sites under the shade of trees. The leaves are semi-evergreen and are heavily splashed and spotted with silver. Clusters of bell-shaped flowers, carried on upright stems, start to appear in late winter and continue through spring, opening purple-pink and then changing to sapphire; both colours are usually seen in each cluster. The new leaves are at their best after the flowers have faded. 'Lewis Palmer' makes a lovely partner for dwarf bulbs and early primroses in a shady corner.

## 12 Sedum 'Herbstfreude'

This sedum is so widely planted that it is easily overlooked when choosing plants for your garden. Forming clumps of upright stems clothed with succulent leaves, it grows to about 40cm (16in) in height. The bold, pale blue-green foliage is welcome throughout the growing season, even before the flattened pink flowerheads open in late summer; these are a rich source of nectar for bees and butterflies. The flowers darken with age to bronze-burgundy by autumn. On well-drained soil they will then turn rich brown, and if they are left in position, they will persist in the winter garden. On damp soils the plant tends to produce rather lush growth, and the stems are likely to collapse in early winter if not supported. This sedum grows best in a sunny border, where it provides months of interest, and both the form of the flowers and their rich colour offer the possibility of pleasing combinations with other plants. Try it alongside purple-leaved heucheras or strappy pink phormiums.

# Guilty pleasures

No matter how hard you try to select your plants for their performance and contribution, you will still be drawn by beauty. We all have our guilty pleasures in life, and the garden is no exception. Those flamboyant characters that bewitch us with their charms are irresistible, even if we know their season is brief. Many flowers from heaven are plants from hell – but you can be allowed just one or two personal indulgences.

1

5

Take the **oriental poppy** for example. It has fantastic large silky blooms that explode from furry buds in early summer, but with one puff of wind or a rainstorm the show is all over for another year. Some varieties are longer-lived and easier to accommodate than others. Of the old favourites *Papaver orientale* 'Patty's Plum' (1) is the best, with soft mauve-grey satin blooms on stout 60cm (2ft) stems that are self-supporting. After flowering it dies back, as all oriental poppies do. Plant it alongside a later performer, like *Echinacea purpurea*, which will take over where the poppy leaves off. Look out for the new varieties of American 'super' poppy: they bloom over a longer period and have longer-lasting flowers. They must have good drainage and plenty of sun.

**Peonies** have a longer season of interest than the perennial poppies. Apart from their sumptuous blooms, they boast beautiful foliage that stays in good condition in the border throughout summer, and may even display autumn colour. Contrary to popular belief peonies are easily transplanted and will establish and bloom successfully, as long as they are not planted too deeply. The top of the rhizome should be no more than a couple of centimetres (about an inch) beneath the soil surface. Peonies rarely need lifting and dividing, and they are long-lived garden plants. Those varieties that produce secondary buds on the flower stems, behind the main flower

bud, will flower for longer. *Paeonia* 'Bowl of Beauty' (2) is a good example, with glorious glowing pink goblet-shaped blooms filled with small creamy-white petals. Enjoying full sun or dappled shade, peonies grow on most soils, love organic matter at their feet, and benefit from some support because of their heavy flowers.

The dreaming spires of **delphiniums** are one of the most irresistible features of the English summer garden, but these are not by any means low-maintenance perennials. Seed-raised delphiniums are usually short-lived garden plants and are best treated as biennials, which means they need

replacing every couple of seasons. The named varieties raised from cuttings can be long-lived if they like your garden. The new shoots of delphiniums are prime fodder for slugs, and the plants always need support. They must be cut back straight after flowering to encourage more flowers to appear in autumn.

If you simply cannot do without delphiniums, then opt for the Belladonna hybrids. These have shorter spikes than the showier Elatum delphiniums and the flowers are not as large, but the colour is intense. Their finely cut foliage and lighter habit make them easier to mix with other plants in the border. *Delphinium*

'Völkerfrieden' (3) is a popular choice, with graceful spikes of deep gentian-blue. All delphiniums need a position in full sun, on fertile, well-drained soil.

From late spring into early summer, the **flag irises** are unsurpassable for the sheer majesty of their blooms. The rest of the year they have miserable untidy foliage usually marked with rust and a host of other diseases. They revel in a sunny position uncluttered with other plants, where their rhizomes can be ripened by the sun. They need lifting and dividing every three years or so, otherwise flowering drops off and the plants deteriorate. *Iris* 'Sultan's Palace' (4) and

*Iris* 'Cantina' (5) are just two of myriad colourways to choose from. If you can find a space, perhaps at the base of a sunny wall, you can delight in their brief beauty and ignore them for the rest of the year. If not, grow varieties of *Iris sibirica* instead. Although the blooms are smaller and more delicate than those of the flag irises, the foliage is fine and adds light spike to the border. The clumps rarely need dividing and maintain an excellent performance for many years.

**Lupins** fall into the same category as delphiniums. One of the quintessential

cottage-garden plants, their dense spikes of gaily coloured flowers, rising from clumps of fresh green foliage in early summer, have a special appeal. The soft yellow *Lupinus* 'Chandelier' (6) is an old favourite. If you really want to grow lupins, they will sulk; if you are indifferent, they will thrive. It is one of the most annoying rules of gardening. They prefer neutral to acid, well-drained soil, and dislike heavy, wet clay. As with delphiniums, cut them hard back after flowering to encourage later blooms, and be prepared to replant every couple of years.

# Perennials for fabulous foliage

Perennials grown for their foliage contribute to the planting picture in a number of ways. Some provide colour with purple or variegated foliage, while others supply variety of form and texture through the shape and character of their leaves. Some add to that all important planting layer at ground level, filling the space beneath taller plants, while others are useful for prolonged interest in pots and containers.

*Brunnera macrophylla* 'Jack Frost' (1) is one of the finest foliage plants. A compact perennial growing to 30cm (12in) in height, it has large, heart-shaped green leaves exquisitely marbled and traced with silver. The foliage is striking from the time the new leaves appear with the first forget-me-not-like blue flowers in early spring. The leaves remain in good condition well into winter. This is a superb perennial for a site in shade or semi-shade and it works well under taller shrubs.

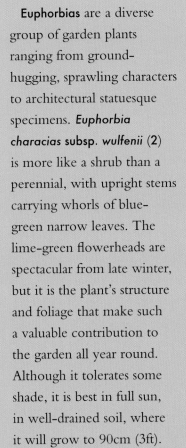

**Euphorbias** are a diverse group of garden plants ranging from ground-hugging, sprawling characters to architectural statuesque specimens. *Euphorbia characias* **subsp.** *wulfenii* (2) is more like a shrub than a perennial, with upright stems carrying whorls of blue-green narrow leaves. The lime-green flowerheads are spectacular from late winter, but it is the plant's structure and foliage that make such a valuable contribution to the garden all year round. Although it tolerates some shade, it is best in full sun, in well-drained soil, where it will grow to 90cm (3ft).

**Heucheras** have taken over from hostas as the most popular foliage perennials today. A few years ago only a handful of varieties were found, usually grown for their spikes of tiny flowers. Now, a host of new cultivars boast exotically beautiful and highly coloured evergreen leaves. Many are useful plants for the border in sun or semi-shade and most make good permanent plants for pots.

*Heuchera* 'Plum Pudding' is one of the best for purple foliage, with large purple leaves that have a slight silver sheen. These are softly waved and carried on 20cm (8in) stalks. *Heuchera* 'Licorice' (3) is darker, shinier and more dramatic. It is slightly smaller than 'Plum Pudding', as is *Heuchera* 'Midnight Rose', a lovely new variety with purple-black leaves finely splashed with cerise-pink. All are tough, easy-to-grow

Although heucheras are easy to grow, they are prone to attack by vine weevils. This is easy to detect by looking for notches around the edge of the leaves (slugs and snails make holes in the middle of the leaf blades as well). Drench the plants with a chemical or biological vine-weevil control in late spring or early autumn. The objective is to kill the larvae that feed on the roots and cause plants to collapse and die.

plants that will give many years of pleasure.

*Heuchera* 'Green Spice' (**4**) has pale green leaves with peridot shading and olive-green veining that becomes more prominent and purple-brown in winter. They form a low mound that looks good in a pot. Of similar size, *Heuchera* 'Crème Brûlée' (**5**) is one of the honey-coloured varieties, with pale amber leaves shaded lilac below. Heucheras of this colouring are nowhere near as hardy as the green- and purple-leaved varieties, and they are harder to fit into planting schemes in the open ground. They do, however, make eyecatching plants for pots, where they enjoy good drainage and some winter protection.

**Hostas** are associated with fabulous foliage, but sadly also with slug and snail damage. If you have a major mollusc problem, then leave hostas alone, or grow them in pots so that you can protect them. The blue-leaved varieties are the least susceptible to damage. They will grow in full sun, but are happiest in semi-shade. *Hosta* 'Blue Wedgwood' (**6**) is relatively

Hostas are easy to grow. They do well on most soils, but they like reasonable moisture and adequate organic matter around their roots. In the open ground mulch with garden compost or well-rotted manure and apply a general fertilizer before the shoots start to emerge in early spring.

compact, rarely reaching 30cm (12in) in height and ultimately 60cm (2ft) in spread. The leaves are gently waved, pointed, and blue-green in colour. Pale lavender flowers appear on stiff spikes above the leaves in summer. *Hosta* 'June' (**7**) is taller, growing to 50cm (20in) high, with leaves of a similar blue-green but with soft yellow centres. This is one of the finest hostas, with foliage that remains in excellent condition throughout the season. Give it a little more sun than other hostas to get the best from the leaf colour.

Anyone who has *Lysimachia ciliata* 'Firecracker' (**8**) in their garden will know that it can be invasive given the opportunity. However, it is still worth growing for its upright stems, up to 90cm (3ft) high, with bronze-purple leaves; these emerge

in spring and are at their best through early summer. It grows on any soil, wet or dry, and mixes well with shrubs and other perennials, where it adds depth to a colour scheme; plant it in full sun for the richest foliage colour.

*Persicaria microcephala* 'Red Dragon' (**9**) is better behaved. It stays in one place, producing sprawling fleshy stems, up to 90cm (3ft) high, with deep bronze-red leaves, beautifully marked with silver. It is at its best in partial shade and likes a reasonable amount of moisture in the soil. It is always knocked back by the first frost.

# Annuals *and* bulbs *Adding extra colour*

Although wonderful effects can be achieved with permanent planting, there are times when most of us crave more colour in our gardens. For that added boost, annuals and bulbs are unbeatable. These provide the exclamation marks of the seasons: cheery spring daffodils and colourful primroses, bright summer geraniums and marigolds, and the early autumn spectacle of dahlias and sunflowers. As the more temporary decorations of the garden, they may be changed annually, and they are an easy way to create exciting planting combinations.

As with all garden plants, some are more rewarding than others. Some bulbs, such as crocus and narcissi, perform year after year, whereas some of the more delicate tulips and hyacinths have a more fleeting presence in most gardens. Some annuals have a short season whereas others go on blooming for weeks.

## Hardy annuals

Gaps in beds and borders offer the ideal opportunity to add colour by sowing hardy annuals such as godetia, clarkia, nigella and clary sage. These are easy to grow and can be sown thinly, directly into the open ground where they are intended to flower. They are particularly useful in areas of new planting before the main shrubs and herbaceous perennials grow to fill the space. With a little care when weeding, they will often self-seed and reappear every year.

## Other annuals and biennials

Other annuals can be started indoors or purchased as young plants and transplanted into spaces in the permanent planting. If you are aiming to make your garden easy maintenance, you do not want to do too much of this, as the process will have to be repeated annually, or twice a year if you choose to plant wallflowers or pansies in the same position in the autumn. You will also have to remove the faded plants at the end of the season.

However, some annuals, such as *Cleome spinosa* and *Cosmos bipinnatus*, have a very long flowering season, from midsummer through to autumn, and fit in well with shrubs and perennials. The cleome has delicate flowers of

**Above**: *Nigella* 'Miss Jekyll', love-in-a-mist, can be sown directly where it is to flower. **Left**: A group of *Tulipa* 'Menton' amid a foam of forget-me-nots injects early colour into a border of shrubs and perennials.

The biggest problem with sowing direct is the annual weed seeds already in the soil. Cultivation brings these to the surface and they germinate and compete with the emerging seedlings of your hardy annuals. The problem can be reduced by sowing into a layer of multi-purpose potting compost spread on the soil surface. This gives your new seedlings ideal growing conditions and helps to bury the weed seeds and stop them from germinating.

Most flower bulbs, and nearly all annuals, require a certain amount of input from you, so they cannot be regarded as maintenance-free. However, they can be very rewarding and they give quick results, with only a few months between planting and flowering.

pink, lilac and white with long stamens, creating a sparkling effect, while the cosmos produces shining yellow-eyed daisies in white and shades of pink, lilac, purple and crimson. Both grow to 60–90cm (2–3ft) high, and three plants in a group will fill a space 90cm (3ft) across in a good year. Although these are relatively large plants, they have a pleasing lightness and daintiness against other planting.

*Salvia farinacea* 'Victoria' is more compact, with narrow dark green leaves and spikes of deep blue flowers from midsummer right through into autumn. Like all blue flowers, it is a great mixer and really useful among earlier-flowering perennials.

Sweet William (*Dianthus barbatus*) is an old cottage-garden favourite, popular for its fragrant, long-lasting flowers, mainly in shades of pink, red and purple; these are carried on stout stems above dark green foliage. It is a biennial, so you need to sow seed in spring or summer for flowers the following year, or buy plants in the autumn. The flower stems of most varieties grow only to around 30cm (12in), so this is a valuable plant for a narrow border. The dark-coloured varieties such as *Dianthus barbatus* Nigrescens Group are particularly attractive and add depth to any planting scheme. Sweet Williams make wonderful cut flowers.

The biennial common honesty, *Lunaria annua*, is great for adding early colour where it can be sown directly into the ground alongside a hedge or under mature shrubs. The bright purple spring flowers are followed by flat green seed pods that turn into shining silvery discs on the dry stems in winter. Honesty thrives in sun or part shade. Likewise, the common foxglove,

*Digitalis purpurea*, grows happily at the back of the border or under the shade of trees.

Honesty and foxgloves are often offered as young plants alongside herbaceous perennials, but remember that these are biennials. In their first year they grow and produce a rosette of leaves. The following year they flower, and then die. They will seed themselves if you let them. Tidy gardeners who cut off the flower spikes as soon as they fade will need to replace the plants with new stock the following season.

See also *Pots: Better summer bedding*, pages 140–143.

Top left: *Cosmos bipinnatus* flowers for many weeks in summer. **Above left**: Sweet William, *Dianthus barbatus,* is fragrant and long-lasting. **Above**: The brilliant purple flowers of honesty, *Lunaria annua*, go on to form flat green pods that turn papery and silver in winter.

If you have only a small garden, it is probably better to buy a few plants of most of your favourite annuals and biennials, rather than growing them from seed. A packet of seeds can produce a lot of plants and, unless you are growing for your neighbours, you will have more than you can use. Reserve your seed-raising efforts for those choice varieties that you cannot find as plants.

There are literally thousands of varieties of plants grown for seasonal bedding and there are many new introductions every year. New varieties are developed for their compact growth habit, freedom of flowering, weather- and disease-resistance, and for their ability to shed their faded blooms (so needing no dead-heading). If you are going to use seasonal bedding plants in your garden, look out for good new varieties. F1 hybrids are usually a pretty safe bet: these have been bred for superior performance.

Some bedding plants, such as bedding begonias and French marigolds, can look decidedly out of place in the border, and in the low-maintenance garden they are best confined to pots and containers.

**Far left**: Early daffodils and snowdrops add colour to a bed before herbaceous perennials get underway. **Left**: *Narcissus* 'Jetfire' is one of the finest dwarf daffodils, ideal for the smaller garden.

Bulbs that are unlikely to perform the following season are best grown in pots (see page 137).

## Flower bulbs

Flower bulbs are enduringly popular. They are easy to buy, plant and grow, and they are reliable. They are a great way to brighten up the garden – both in spring, when they deliver that wake-up call after the dull days of winter, and in summer, when beds and borders can run out of steam.

Despite the fact that flower bulbs are inexpensive to buy, and choosing them is an annual ritual for most of us, there is a tendency to expect too much of them. Many gardeners think a bulb is for life, not just for the spectacular display it produces in its first year. Some go through the rigmarole of lifting their bulbs, drying them and storing them for the following season. This really is not worth the effort, as they rarely perform as well. If you do lift your bulbs after flowering, transplant them to the compost heap and start again next year; this is particularly important in a small garden, where every plant has a significant role and needs always to put on a good show.

## Spring bulbs for permanent planting

Not all bulbs are one-hit wonders. Some spring-flowering bulbs can be left in the ground and will repeat year after year. Most will multiply, either by seeding themselves or making larger clumps by producing offsets. These can be considered as any other perennial garden plant; the beauty of them is that they perform before most herbaceous subjects get going.

### Daffodils and narcissi

Daffodils and narcissi suit our climate and thrive on just about any soil. Their biggest drawback is how slowly their foliage dies down after flowering; and you must leave it in place if you want the bulbs to flower well the following year. Traditional large-flowered daffodils and narcissi may make a lovely show when they are in bloom, but they certainly look awful after flowering. This is not a problem in a large garden, but in a small plot you should avoid them. Instead, choose the dwarf varieties, which grow to

Daffodils and narcissi need to be planted where their fading leaves will not detract from the garden. If you are thinking of naturalizing them in grass, bear in mind that you will have to leave the grass uncut until the bulb foliage starts to yellow and die down. They are useful towards the centre of beds and borders, under deciduous shrubs that come into leaf later in spring. They are most effective, and easiest to manage, if you plant them in groups of 10–15, leaving about 5cm (2in) between the bulbs to give them space to multiply. Plant the bulbs at three or four times their own depth; shallow planting can result in stunted growth and poor performance.

around 20–30cm (8–12in) in height and have narrower leaves.

Narcissus 'Jetfire' is one of the finest dwarf daffodils. The golden yellow blooms have swept-back petals and bright orange trumpets. Lasting for three weeks or more, they are rain-resistant and survive a buffeting by the wind. Narcissus 'Jack Snipe' is similar in stature but has creamy-white petals and pale yellow trumpets.

If you want a plain yellow dwarf daffodil then grow Narcissus 'February Gold', with its elegantly poised blooms and dark green foliage. Double daffodils are best avoided in any garden: the stems nearly always bend and break under the weight of the flowers. Narcissus 'Pencrebar' is an exception, with delicate, deep yellow double blooms, which are deliciously scented.

## Tulips

Tulips hail from the eastern Mediterranean so they like warmer, drier conditions than many English gardens offer. On heavy clay soils they often fail to reappear after the first season. On lighter, warmer soils, especially sand, the more vigorous types may perform for many years.

If you want them to last, choose the strong Darwin hybrids, or single early or late tulips. Double and parrot tulips tend to be more delicate; they are also less weather-resistant and can be damaged by wind and heavy rain. Some of the stronger species and species hybrids are also good long-term garden plants, especially when planted in gravel or scree.

It is easy to be bewitched by the exotic images of tulip blooms on bulb packets: they are some of the most striking flowers in terms of variety of shape and colour. If you want them to work in the garden, you need to choose carefully, to make sure they will fit into the existing planting. Strong reds can be difficult, and yellows are often overpowered by the volume of daffodils around at the same time. Orange tulips are a guilty pleasure for some, and loathed by others; however, this is a welcome colour in the spring garden, paired with early blue flowers like pulmonaria and forget-me-not. Deep purple, mauve and soft

**Above left:** Narcissus 'February Gold' has graceful flowers and fine foliage. **Above:** Narcissus 'Jack Snipe' and Narcissus 'Pencrebar' make a fresh and fragrant show under a birch tree.

Never plant tulips too early: delay until November or even December. Early planting can result in early growth that is susceptible to tulip fire, a destructive disease that will prevent you growing tulips in the ground for several years. Always plant the biggest, best-quality bulbs you can find, but bear in mind that size does vary according to type and variety. Plant them at three or more times their own depth. Tall tulips can be planted in small groups in the border, or they can be planted individually and sprinkled through the planting.

Top: The sleek, satin blooms of *Tulipa* 'Queen of Night'. **Above:** The elegant lily-flowered *Tulipa* 'White Triumphator'. **Right**: *Tulipa* 'Ballerina' is bold but very graceful.

Plant allium bulbs in autumn, in well-drained soil, either singly or in small groups. Space the bulbs of larger-blooming varieties at least 15cm (6in) apart to show off the individual form of the flowers. Plant the bulbs at three or four times their own depth.

pink are easy to fit into most gardens. Flamed and striped flowers are accent blooms; plant them as focal points to draw attention.

*Tulipa* 'Queen of Night' – known as the 'black tulip' – is one of the best for the garden and has stood the test of time. The long-lasting single blooms are purple-black with an exquisite silky sheen to the petals; they are carried on stems up to 60cm (2ft) high and appear in late April. Plant it on its own or mix it with any other colour tulip that blooms at the same time. It makes a dramatic partnership with the single white *Tulipa* 'Maureen', and tones perfectly with the soft mauve and white *Tulipa* 'Shirley'. *Tulipa* 'Menton' (see page 128) is also a good choice: the flowers are goblets of pale pink

with a hint of orange, particularly at the edge of the petals. *Tulipa* 'Dordogne' is a sport of 'Menton', with stronger-coloured blooms that are more of a rich salmon and orange. Both are long-lasting and reliable.

Lily-flowered tulips are tall and elegant with pointed petals. *Tulipa* 'Ballerina' is one of the earliest of these, usually opening in mid-April. The beautifully poised flowers are glowing orange and are carried on 60cm (2ft) stems. *Tulipa* 'White Triumphator' is pure white, and is slightly taller and later than 'Ballerina'.

Tulips of the Viridiflora Group are both subtle and graceful. Pointed buds open to butterfly-like blooms, usually with pointed petals, each with a streak of green at the base. *Tulipa* 'Spring Green' is delightful, with green and white flowers, and looks lovely among the fresh emerging leaves of perennials. *Tulipa* 'Groenland' (Greenland) has open blooms of pink, gold and green. Both of these flower late, towards the end of April, and grow to about 50cm (20in) high.

## Alliums

Bridging the gap between spring and summer, alliums flower in May and June, their striking spherical flowerheads bouncing across the border. The shape of the flowers is their unique selling point; it is quite unlike anything else in the garden. In shades of mauve, purple and occasionally white, they fit in easily with other plants. They are the magic ingredient that makes an ordinary border into a showpiece.

Most alliums have very poor foliage that starts to shrivel and fade as the blooms open. For best effect, position them where the leaves and lower part of the stem will be hidden by other planting. They work well among herbaceous geraniums and *Alchemilla mollis*, and they make superb companions for low-growing silver foliage shrubs, such as helichrysum, santolina and artemisia.

*Allium cristophii* is the best of all the alliums. Growing up to 60cm (2ft) in height, it has light and open spherical heads, 15–20cm (6–8in) across, of silver-mauve, starry flowers that shine like sparklers in the border. The flowers are long-lasting and fade to green seedheads that eventually turn to parchment. These persist in the border right into winter and are marvellous for cutting. *Allium schubertii* has even larger flowerheads, with tiny silvery mauve flowers on longer stalks radiating from the top of the flower stem. It is intriguing, dramatic and beautiful, particularly when planted with light airy grasses such as *Stipa tenuissima*.

*Allium sphaerocephalum* is one of the latest to bloom. It has small, compact flowerheads of mauve and dark purple, on tall slender stems up to 90cm (3ft) high. It takes up no space and adds colour and interest anywhere in the summer garden.

## Dwarf bulbs

There are a host of spring-flowering dwarf bulbs that add colour in those nooks and crannies where other plants fear to raise their heads: around the base of a tree, in cracks in paving, at the foot of a hedge, under deciduous shrubs, and alongside paths and patios. These are detail plants that reward year after year.

Crocus are the most obvious choice, but the flowers can be very short-lived; the large-

flowered varieties are easily damaged by weather and never die gracefully. Choose the smaller-flowered species and their hybrids. These have fine foliage that dies down quickly and they look more natural when planted in grass or gravel. *Chionodoxa forbesii*, with its starry blue and white flowers and fresh green leaves, is particularly valuable in shade and under trees. *Ipheion uniflorum*, with blue or white blooms, is a useful little treasure to tuck in alongside paved areas or in gaps between paving stones.

*Anemone blanda* is a wonderful plant, especially the blue-flowered variety with its dark green foliage and starry blue, yellow-eyed flowers. Growing to only 10cm (4in) high, it fits in anywhere. Soak the corms for 24 hours prior to planting in autumn, and weed carefully where you have this anemone planted because it spreads by seeding itself and the tiny seedlings are easily missed.

Snowdrops, perhaps our favourite early spring flowers, are trickier to establish than many dwarf bulbs. They are best planted in

**Above:** The curiously spiky bloom of *Allium schubertii*. **Left:** *Allium cristophii*. **Below:** *Chionodoxa forbesii*. **Below centre:** *Ipheion* 'Rolf Fiedler'. **Bottom:** *Anemone blanda* will seed itself if you let it.

Above: A carpet of *Cyclamen hederifolium*. **Bottom left**: *Eranthis hyemalis*. **Bottom right**: Snowdrops, *Galanthus nivalis*, are always a delight in late winter.

Lilies are greedy feeders so must have fertile soil; they also need good drainage. Plant them as soon as you buy them in autumn or early spring. Plant in groups of three or five, and cover the bulbs with soil to three or four times their depth. Lay the bulbs on their sides to prevent water lodging between the bulb scales and causing them to rot.

early autumn, or better still 'in the green' in early spring, straight after flowering. *Galanthus nivalis* dislikes hot, dry conditions; it likes semi-shade and a reasonably moist soil.

Around the base of trees, *Cyclamen hederifolium* is an excellent choice. Although its pink or white flowers do not appear until autumn, its marbled leaves form a prettily patterned carpet in winter and spring. It works well planted with the winter aconite, *Eranthis hyemalis*, which has ruffs of green foliage and golden yellow flowers in late winter. The new seed-raised *Cyclamen hederifolium* 'Amaze Me' is particularly fine. It establishes easily, clumps up quickly and flowers from July to October.

## Summer-flowering bulbs

Summer-flowering bulbs, corms and tubers are often overlooked as a wonderful source of inexpensive plant material that can really pack a punch in the summer and autumn garden. Some, such as the large-flowered gladioli, are difficult to site, and are best confined to the allotment or vegetable patch for use as cut flowers. Some of the larger dahlias are labour intensive, needing staking and pinching out as well as dead-heading. However, there are plenty of good lilies and smaller dahlias that are really useful garden plants. Cannas, callas, eucomis and other exotics could find a place in pots on your patio.

## Lilies

Lilies are a good way to add light height, a different flower form and, most importantly, fragrance to the summer garden. Stiff, upright, dwarf varieties with upward-facing flowers are fine as indoor pot plants, or in containers on the patio, but they look out of place among perennials and shrubs in the border. Elegant trumpet-flowered lilies and those with reflexed petals fit in beautifully – and the situation suits them perfectly, as their roots receive welcome shade from neighbouring plants, while their tops are in the sun.

There are many excellent hybrid lilies to choose from, but the regal lily, *Lilium regale*, still reigns supreme as queen of the summer garden. The elegant trumpet blooms open in midsummer and are shining white within, with yellow into the throat of the flower, while the outside of the petals is flushed with purple-pink. With their strong stems and narrow dark green

leaves they are less susceptible to attack by lily beetle than are the oriental hybrids, which have broader, fleshy leaves. *Lilium regale* grows up to 1.2m (4ft) high.

*Lilium speciosum* var. *rubrum* flowers in late summer. It grows to 90cm (3ft), and has elegant downward-facing flowers with reflexed petals of white, heavily flushed deep pink and spotted with deep red. It makes an exotic planting partner for the flattened pink flowerheads of *Sedum* 'Herbstfreude', which appear at the same time. *Lilium henryi* is another late bloomer, with tall stems carrying soft orange flowers with reflexed petals. It works well with grasses and late prairie plants such as rudbeckia and echinacea. *Lilium* Golden Splendor Group is an old trumpet-flowered variety growing to 1.2m (4ft) or more in height. The fragrant, old gold flowers open in mid- to late summer.

## Dahlias

You can grow dahlias from tubers, purchased in early spring and started in pots indoors, or planted out in late spring directly where they are intended to flower. Alternatively, you can buy them as pot-grown plants later on. All do well on fertile, well-drained soil. The most useful varieties are those with single flowers, or the pom-poms and small-flowered decorative and cactus types. These mix easily with other plants, where large-bloomed varieties would look out of place. Those with dark chocolate or bronze foliage add an extra dimension to the planting and so are particularly valuable.

*Dahlia* 'Bishop of Llandaff', with dark foliage and bright red flowers, has become one of those essential garden plants. It grows to 1.2m (4ft)

in height and adds vibrant colour to the late summer garden. Where it is too tall, choose the more compact *Dahlia* 'Tally Ho'. *Dahlia* 'Roxy', with vivid purple flowers, and *Dahlia* 'Moonfire', with amber and orange blooms, are perhaps even more arresting.

In the same way that dark tulips have become popular, so have dark wine-red and purple dahlias. The sumptuous *Dahlia* 'Arabian Night', growing to 1.2m (4ft) high, has black-red blooms tightly packed with petals. The new *Dahlia* 'Karma Choc' is even richer in hue and has the advantage of bronze foliage; it is slightly shorter in stature, at 90cm (3ft) high. It would make a wonderful planting partner for bright orange crocosmias and the tiny purple and orange blooms of *Verbena bonariensis*.

**Top left:** *Lilium* Golden Splendor Group, a lovely trumpet lily. **Top right:** The deliciously fragrant *Lilium regale*. **Above left:** *Dahlia* 'Bishop of Llandaff'. **Above:** The bright and cheerful *Dahlia* 'Moonfire'.

Traditionally dahlias are lifted when the foliage is knocked down by the first frosts. The tubers are then stored in a frost-free place in boxes of dry potting compost or sand, and started into growth the following spring. With milder winters most gardeners now leave them in the ground and let them take their chance. Given a good mulch of chipped bark, they are fairly certain to survive unharmed.

# Pots *and* containers *The essentials*

**Left**: A variety of foliage form and texture and a sprinkling of flowers are pleasing to look at and easy to maintain. **Below**: Fragrant heliotrope is a delight for a pot in a sunny spot. **Below centre**: Gravel and carefully arranged pebbles make a feature on the compost surface. **Bottom**: The metallic foliage of *Heuchera* 'Licorice' looks perfect in a glazed pot.

There is no denying the colourful impact of bedding plants in pots and hanging baskets. However, if you have quite a few they will involve a lot of replanting, a lot of maintenance and considerable expenditure year after year. A more impressive and lasting display can be achieved with permanent plants in pots, in conjunction with containers of spring bulbs and some seasonal bedding to add variety and colour. Grouping containers together is more effective than having single pots dotted here and there, and it gives you the opportunity to try different combinations of pots and plants to achieve the most pleasing result.

## Permanent planting in pots

Shrubs, perennials, ferns, grasses, conifers and even small trees can be grown in pots long-term. They do not necessarily need re-potting every year or so. With the right container and compost, and annual feeding with a controlled-release fertilizer, many will do perfectly well in the same container for a number of years.

Slow-growing plants are the obvious choice if you want them to be happy in the same pot for several years. However, the most important consideration is the size and shape of the plant in relation to the container. Timescale is a more critical factor when choosing a plant for a pot than when choosing one for the open

Always choose good-quality pots, and buy the largest you can for permanent subjects. Well-made English terracotta pots are usually the best; they may cost more than imported ones, but will last longer.

Consider shape: pots that narrow at the neck may look attractive, but it is virtually impossible to extract a well-rooted plant when you come to re-pot it. Choose traditional flowerpot shapes for ease of watering and re-potting.

Always use loam-based potting compost for permanent planting. It holds on to water and nutrients more successfully than soil-less compost, so you need to water less frequently. It is also heavier, so your pots are less likely to blow over.

Put a generous layer of drainage material, ideally broken crocks, in the bottom of the pot to keep the drainage hole open and prevent waterlogging. When the pot sits on a solid surface, use pieces of tile or pot feet to raise it slightly. This prevents the drainage hole becoming blocked, which can result in a cracked pot if the compost is wet and it freezes.

Remember that containers with permanent planting need watering all through the year, even in winter if conditions are dry. Pay particular attention to pots that sit under the eaves.

ground. Usually you want your plant in a pot to look good straight away. If it is far too small for the container, and needs to put on a couple of years' growth before the scale of plant and container works, then it is not the right plant for the pot you are thinking of using.

## One plant to each pot

When growing permanent plants in pots it is generally better to give each one its own individual pot, rather than combining two or three different plants in the same container. If you have two or three dwarf shrubs sharing the same large container, you will meet a problem when you come to re-pot: you will have to rip the plants apart, damaging roots and branches to separate them. If they are grown in individual containers, you can just slip each plant out, keeping the rootball intact, and transfer it to a larger pot.

You can achieve the effect of mixed planting by grouping containers together. In large pots you can underplant the main subject with a ground-cover plant, just as you would in the open ground. Ivies and ajugas are useful beneath larger specimen shrubs, providing they are kept under control and are not allowed to smother the main plant.

## Bulbs and seasonal bedding in pots

When you are growing plants that will occupy the pot for only one season and then be discarded, you can be more relaxed about the shape of container that you use. It will not be necessary to get the rootball out intact, so pots that become narrower at the neck will not cause a problem.

You should still use good-quality potting compost: a mixture of two-thirds multi-purpose compost and one-third John Innes No.3 is ideal for most subjects. Cheap soil-less composts generally give poorer results: they contain fewer nutrients and usually dry out more quickly.

Add controlled-release fertilizer at the time of planting. This feeds the plants over a long period. Regular watering washes away the nutrients plants need, so these must be replenished regularly. Soluble and liquid feeds, applied with a watering can, are an alternative, but will give you yet another thing to think about during the growing season. Using a controlled-release fertilizer takes away all the hassle.

## Plant, pot and finishing touches

Finding the right pot for a plant, and vice versa, is a creative process, and often one of trial and error: get the combination right and you will have a work of art that will give you a glow of pleasure every time you look at it. Choose pots that suit your garden and the plants you want to grow in them. Appropriateness is key: do not be drawn by any other factor, least of all price.

Attention to detail makes all the difference. Covering the compost with stone chippings, pebbles, ceramic beads or crushed glass insulates the surface, conserving moisture and suppressing weed seedlings. It also completes the picture, showing off both container and plant to full advantage.

See also *Trees in pots*, pages 86–87 and *Small shrubs for pots*, pages 94–95.

# Pots   *Grasses, ferns and bamboos*

Top: Silky *Stipa tenuissima* in a blue glazed pot. **Centre**: The delicate blooms of *Tulipa* 'Lady Jane' among the blue blades of *Festuca glauca*. **Above**: Early crocus brave the snow among the gold and green leaves of *Carex oshimensis* 'Evergold'.

Pots are an excellent way to showcase the form and texture of foliage. In both traditional and contemporary settings, ferns, grasses and bamboos can provide year-round interest. Grown in pots they make terrific partners for containers of bulbs; both the feathery foliage of ferns and the sharp but soft lines of grasses and bamboos contrast with the bright, satiny blooms of crocus, elegant narcissi and sleek tulips.

## Grasses

Some dwarf bulbs with fine foliage can be grown in the same pots as short grasses such as *Festuca glauca*. *Tulipa clusiana*, for example, enjoys the same well-drained conditions and copes well with summer drought; it will perform for several years alongside the grass. It has the same blue-grey foliage, and leaves behind seedheads that enhance the festuca. The tulip blooms in mid-spring, with slender buds opening to starry flowers with pointed petals. The cultivar 'Lady Jane' has shining petals, which are soft pink on the outside of the flower, white within.

Species crocus also have unobtrusive, grass-like leaves and can be tucked in around grasses and sedges, where they add cheery early colour, well before any pansies or violas wake up in the spring. Try *Crocus chrysanthus* 'E.A. Bowles', which is rich lemon yellow with bronze at the base, or the lovely *Crocus chrysanthus* 'Cream Beauty' with golden *Carex oshimensis* 'Evergold'.

There are both deciduous and evergreen ornamental grasses. Evergreens are the obvious choice for pots, and they really come into their own in winter, especially in low sunlight and when their fine leaves are etched by frost. *Carex comans* bronze-leaved is one of the most widely planted, but it is a plant that you either love or hate. Its copper-brown foliage delights some of us, and appears dead to others. It does not work particularly well with green foliage, but looks wonderful with copper and purple heucheras or on its own in terracotta or salt-glazed pots.

*Carex comans* 'Frosted Curls', on the other hand, has wide appeal. Its gently arching leaves are soft peridot green and drape gently over the edge of a pot.

Larger grasses for pots need to be self-supporting. Choose the clump-forming varieties with stiffer leaves, or soft silky ones that form a tidy mound. *Elymus magellanicus* has striking upright leaves of light steely blue, with even more intensely coloured flower spikes rising above the foliage in summer. *Stipa tenuissima* is an easy grass that seeds itself on sandy soils. Its fine hair-like leaves mix beautifully with other plants in a sunny position. In a container it is almost smoke-like and is fun to grow in an old chimney pot.

*Pennisetum setaceum* 'Rubrum' is one of the most beautiful grasses for pots. Sadly, it is not hardy, but it is well worth the effort of planting anew each year. The leaves are ruby red, the colour becoming more intense as the season progresses. The flower spikes grow to 60cm (2ft) or so and arch gracefully, each terminating in a long, fluffy seedhead.

All of the grasses mentioned here need an open, sunny position, but the sedges (Carex) will tolerate a little shade.

## Ferns

Ferns are an excellent choice for pots in shade. There are deciduous and evergreen varieties; both can be grown in containers, but the evergreens will provide interest through the winter months. There are hundreds of different ferns to choose from, each with its own unique leaf form and pattern.

Some prefer an acid soil, so lime-free John Innes is the best compost to choose; most will be happy in the same pot for many years if a little controlled-release fertilizer is applied annually. Because the root systems of most ferns remain fairly compact, you can grow them in smaller containers and more unusually shaped pots than you would choose for other permanent subjects that might need re-potting.

*Polystichum polyblepharum*, the Japanese tassel fern, is a wonderful choice for a container. The finely divided, evergreen fronds are shiny on the upper surface, with glistening golden brown scales along the central leaf-stalk. The leaves form a beautiful open shuttlecock.

*Polystichum setiferum* Divisilobum Group 'Herrenhausen' is particularly elegant, with

long feathered evergreen fronds that sweep horizontally from the centre of the plant. It is lovely in a shady corner, in a spot where you can look down into the centre of the plant.

Hart's tongue fern, *Asplenium scolopendrium*, is quite different. The fronds are broad and strap shaped and particularly striking as they unfurl. It is another evergreen and loves shade, but it prefers alkaline soil so grow this one in a pot of John Innes No.3.

## Bamboos

Bamboos are often recommended for pots and containers and they can be very attractive grown in this way. However, once they start to decline they do so very quickly, and this often happens if they dry out in summer. Some of the dwarf bamboos are at their best in semi-shade, sheltered from cold winds, where they can be kept regularly watered.

*Pleioblastus viridistriatus* is one of the most reliable, growing to around 1m (3ft) in a pot; it has fine canes and dark green leaves, strongly striped with bright yellow.

*Pleioblastus variegatus* is similar in stature, with cream-striped leaves carried on slender canes. It can be cut back in spring to encourage new growth if the old foliage looks tatty.

**Above left:** *Asplenium scolopendrium*, the hart's tongue fern. **Above:** The vibrant dwarf bamboo *Pleioblastus viridistriatus* in an oriental glazed pot.
**Below left:** *Polystichum polyblepharum*: stunning throughout the year in semi-shade.
**Below:** The graceful feather-like fronds of *Polystichum setiferum* 'Herrenhausen'.

# Pots *Better summer bedding*

**Top left**: *Verbena* 'Aztec Red Velvet'.
**Top right**: *Sutera* 'Copia Great Blue Lake'. **Above**: The stunning variegated foliage and striking flowers of *Fuchsia* 'Firecracker'.

*Plectranthus caninus* and *Plectranthus ornatus* 'Pee Off' have become popular for their aromatic foliage, which is supposedly repellent to cats. They are widely planted in the hope of keeping gardens cat-free. By all means give these a go, but do not be surprised to find your cat, and others, bonding with them.

Even if you have lots of permanently planted pots you will probably still want to fill one or two with summer-flowering bedding plants, just to give the garden a boost after those early summer flowers have faded. There is a bewildering number of different varieties to choose from. However, because summer bedding plants are such a traditional garden ingredient, it is easy to fall into the trap of growing the same old things year after year. Perhaps you could do better?

## The attraction of newcomers

There are always plenty of new arrivals each season, and bedding, just like any other plant group, has its fashions and trends. Some plants become outdated because their performance is surpassed by new discoveries that bloom for longer, regardless of what the weather throws at them. Take trailing lobelia for example. A few years ago no hanging basket or patio pot would be without it. Yet it is a delicate plant that can run out of steam halfway through the summer, particularly if allowed to dry out. Trailing verbena, on the other hand, keeps going in

dry conditions and gives a far longer season of colour. New varieties like *Verbena* 'Aztec Red Velvet' have outstanding depth of colour and, because they are such tough, drought-resistant plants, they demand much less attention, which is particularly useful if you subject them to cultivation in a hanging basket.

## Choosing the right plants

As with any garden plant, it is important to choose the right plant for the right situation. For pots in full sun opt for drought-resistant sun-lovers such as zonal pelargoniums (geraniums) and gazanias. In shadier sites choose impatiens, fuchsias or foliage plants, which do not require direct sunlight for flower formation.

Simple combinations of two or three well-chosen varieties that work together in terms of colour and texture are far more effective than containers planted with a great variety of different plants. As in the border, foliage holds a scheme together, and there are some interesting and striking foliage plants in today's bedding selection.

## A few of the best bedding flowers

*Bacopa*, now known as *Sutera*, has become one of the most popular trailing plants in recent years, perhaps because of its tidy habit and dainty flowers and leaves. The stems are clothed in apple-green foliage and tiny white, mauve or blue flowers, and it blooms continuously from early summer through to late autumn. *Sutera cordata* 'Snowflake' is the well-known variety that has been around for a few years. New improved strains with larger flowers are worth looking out for; examples are *Sutera* 'Copia

Gulliver White' and *Sutera* 'Copia Great Blue Lake'. Bacopa is useful because it tolerates a little shade; with its fresh, frothy appearance, it looks especially pleasing alongside water, perhaps with a collection of hostas in pots.

It is hard to beat begonias for situations in shade or semi-shade. They flower with remarkable continuity, and their fleshy-petalled flowers are exceptionally weather-resistant, even more so than those of impatiens.

Begonias grown from tubers can be spectacular, but they do have the disadvantage that you need to start them indoors. Also, they do not always produce many stems, so they are more vulnerable to damage during the course of the growing season. The ones you buy as plants are grown from plugs and these can be planted straight out after danger of frost has passed. They normally produce many-stemmed plants that flower prolifically. *Begonia* Illumination Series is a free-flowering alternative to *Begonia* Pendula Group, grown from tubers. The flowers are bright, beautiful and weather-resistant.

*Begonia* 'Million Kisses' is an even daintier alternative, with semi-double hanging flowers with narrow petals. The original variety has glowing orange-coral flowers, and the newer 'Million Kisses Elegance' has bronze-tinged foliage and soft cream, salmon-flushed flowers. It is delightful grown in a terracotta pot or in a wicker hanging basket.

Diascias are hardier plants, despite their fine thread-like stems and plentiful tiny flowers. They will sometimes establish as permanent subjects in sheltered positions. Thriving in a sunny spot, they are ideal planted to creep over

the edge of patio containers, and are especially effective in shallow bowls. *Diascia barberae* 'Ruby Field' has been one of the most popular varieties for many years; its soft mauve-pink flowers typify the hues associated with these plants. Brighter colours are now appearing on the scene. *Diascia* 'Wink Orange' is one of the new generation, with vibrant orange flowers produced in profusion. It makes an exciting partner for bright blues and purples, such as those found in the range of calibrachoa varieties (see page 143).

Everyone loves gazanias – their open single flowers just radiate sunshine. These are well-behaved plants that stay close to the ground, producing a clump of green or grey leaves and individual flowers that smile upwards when open. They love a dry, sunny spot and so are well suited to pots on a sun-drenched patio and are ideal in coastal gardens. Those in the Kiss Series have exceptionally bright, showy flowers with broad petals and bold markings. *Gazania* 'Kiss Orange Flame' is just one of a whole range of vibrant hot colours that are well worth growing.

**Top left**: *Diascia* 'Wink Orange'. **Top right**: *Gazania* 'Kiss Orange Flame'. **Above**: *Begonia* 'Million Kisses Elegance' lives up to its name and is excellent in a hanging pot or basket.

**Top left:** *Osteospermum* 'Asti'. **Top right:** *Nemesia* 'Aromatica True Blue'. **Centre:** *Petunia* 'Fanfare Lime'. **Above:** The fragrant double flowers of *Petunia* (Tumbelina) 'Priscilla' are sure to please.

For those who like daisies but want something taller than gazanias, osteospermums are an obvious choice. These are bushy plants usually growing to around 60cm (2ft) in height. They need full sun to flower well. Provide it and you will be rewarded with a magnificent display of shining daisy blooms in subtle or vibrant colours. These tend to be in the pink, purple, white range, although gorgeous shades of soft yellow and copper also exist. *Osteospermum* 'Asti' is a new variety, typical of the best of these excellent plants.

For smaller daisies on low mat-forming plants look to sanvitalia and brachyscome. *Sanvitalia* 'Spirit' has tiny sunflower-like blooms, golden yellow with dark eyes, carried on creeping stems. It is charming and performs well in a sunny position. Its colour makes it a good partner for gazanias and red or orange geraniums. There are many different varieties of brachyscome. These have fine, feathery foliage and dainty narrow-petalled flowers of blue, white, yellow or mauve. They need a warm sunny position to do well, but do not like to dry out completely.

*Nemesia* Aromatica Series is a lovely spreading plant, not quite trailing but with a graceful habit. The tiny snapdragon-like flowers are clustered towards the tips of softly ascending stems that grow to around 20cm (8in) high. There are forms with white, mauve, pink, purple and blue flowers, often with yellow eyes. Many have a soft, sweet perfume and these are especially welcome planted next to a garden seat. Some will overwinter outdoors in milder areas. *Nemesia* 'Aromatica True Blue' is a good variety, with flowers as the name describes. *Nemesia* 'Amelie' is soft mother-of-pearl pink with a delightful old-fashioned character and superb fragrance; it has a particularly long flowering period, continuing well into autumn.

*Petunia* Surfinia Series has become the staple of commercial and domestic bedding displays in recent years. This vigorous, cutting-raised plant produces long trailing stems, and flowers from early summer until the first frosts. It has two drawbacks. First, it is very strong-growing and takes over if planted with other subjects. Second, it tends to become very straggly and bare towards the base. To avoid this you need to cut it back halfway through the season; few gardeners do this because it means that you lose the flowers for two or three weeks while the plant regrows.

*Petunia* Fanfare Series is better than *Petunia* Surfinia. It is a tidier, more compact plant showing good weather tolerance and resistance to mildew. It is raised from cuttings so you need to buy new plants annually. *Petunia* 'Fanfare Red' is the best of the reds; 'Fanfare Lime' is a gentler alternative, with softly waved flowers of lime yellow. *Petunia* Fanfare is an ideal choice for a pot on a sunny doorstep.

*Petunia* Tumbelina Series is a trailing petunia that produces plenty of fragrant double blooms over a long period. *Petunia* 'Priscilla' is the established favourite, with pale mauve, heavily veined and ruffled blooms. *Petunia* 'Joanna' is a newer pink introduction, and *Petunia* 'Susanna' a soft greenish yellow, which makes it an excellent mixer with just about any other colour you might choose. It is also a subtle, sophisticated plant to grow as the summer-flowering interest in a garden predominantly planted with foliage.

For smaller flowers choose *Calibrachoa*, usually referred to as 'Million Bells'. This is a neat, compact, trailing plant, with small leaves and trumpet flowers that come in a wide range of colours, all with bright yellow throats. It grows and blooms best in full sun where it will produce its flowers prolifically and with wonderful continuity. *Calibrachoa* 'Cabaret Purple' has marvellous depth of colour and makes a striking planting partner for hot reds, oranges and yellows. *Calibrachoa* 'Million Bells Lavender' is softer of hue and mixes well with pinks, mauves and silvers.

## Plants for summer foliage

Many half-hardy plants, once grown as houseplants, are now valued for their foliage in the garden, especially in containers. Until a few years ago, the only seasonal foliage plants available for containers were trailing nepeta and the wiry-stemmed silver *Helichrysum petiolare*. Today there are plenty to choose from and these can be used either as an addition to a flowering

container, or with other foliage plants to create an exciting but subtle combination.

Various types of ipomoea are grown for this purpose. *Ipomoea batatas* 'Margarita' has lime-yellow heart-shaped leaves on slowly trailing stems, producing a compact plant of intense colour. It is a good partner for yellow begonias or pale lime petunias. *Ipomoea batatas* 'Blackie' is equally excellent, with broadly divided leaves of purple-black. Give them a sunny site for best results.

Silver foliage plants are always popular, especially for containers in full sun. *Plectranthus* 'Silver Shield' is particularly good, with stout upright stems and large silver, velvety leaves. It needs pinching back early in the season to keep the plants bushy. It grows well in sun or semi-shade, and it makes a striking partner for white impatiens.

*Strobilanthes* 'Persian Shield' is an exceptional summer foliage plant. The long, narrow and pointed leaves are deep mauve, silver and green, with a wonderful metallic sheen. This plant is sure to attract attention, particularly when combined with partners in pink and silver. It fares best when grown in good light, with shade from direct sun.

Coleus (now *Solenostemon*), a favourite houseplant of the 1960s, has made a comeback and is now widely used in containers outdoors. *Solenostemon* Kong Series has enormous velvety leaves in rich, extravagant colours; it is lovely, but not for the garden. The Wizard Series, on the other hand, has smaller leaves and a compact growth habit and is great for containers on a sunny patio. Pinch out the flowers as they develop to keep the plants looking good.

**Top**: *Calibrachoa* 'Cabaret Purple'.
**Centre**: *Plectranthus* 'Silver Shield'.
**Above**: *Solenostemon* 'Wizard Coral Surprise' is a superb foliage plant for a container on the patio.

# Pots *Winter into spring*

## Winter evergreens

A number of shrubs are grown as small plants for use in patio pots. The ever-popular *Euonymus fortunei* 'Emerald Gaiety', with white and green variegated foliage, and *Euonymus fortunei* 'Emerald 'n' Gold', with rich gold variegation to its dark green leaves, are old favourites. They make excellent additions to pots planted with early-flowering narcissi such as *Narcissus* 'Tête-à-Tête', with deep yellow flowers, and *Narcissus* 'Spring Dawn', with pale yellow and white blooms. *Lonicera nitida* 'Baggesen's Gold' adds smaller, lighter gold leaves carried on light, feathery branches.

For silver foliage, *Santolina chamaecyparissus* and *Helichrysum italicum* both remain in good condition over winter in containers because they enjoy good drainage. Variegated thymes appreciate this, too, and thrive in pots in an open, sunny position. The white-variegated *Thymus pulegioides* 'Foxley' is attractive as the foliage tinges pinkish red at the tips of the shoots. *Thymus* 'Doone Valley' is another excellent variety, with dark green leaves, irregularly edged and blotched with gold.

In shadier situations the small-leaved variegated ivies are indispensable. They are rarely sold as named varieties; select according to whatever combination of colour and leaf shape takes your fancy. Ajugas succeed in sun or shade during the winter months. The shining foliage is striking and colourful, and there is the bonus of sapphire flowers to look forward to in spring. *Ajuga reptans* 'Burgundy Glow' is a lovely variety, with leaves of burgundy, pink, cream and green. Where a larger plant and bolder leaves are required,

**Above:** This corner is brought to life in winter with evergreen shrubs and perennials and a few little treasures in terracotta pots. **Below:** A group of primroses in shades of orange has real impact – far more than the same pot filled with a mixture of colours.

There is no reason to leave pots and containers empty and forlorn during the winter and spring, just to await their annual replant with summer bedding. A wide variety of perennials, small shrubs, conifers, heathers and grasses are available in small pots to bring evergreen interest to patio containers during the winter months. In addition pansies, violas, primulas and cyclamen promise flowers before spring bulbs appear. A cluster of well-planted containers brings the garden nearer to the house, so you can enjoy them from the windows when the weather is too cold and wet for you to be tempted outdoors.

**Right:** *Pinus mugo* 'Winter Gold' underplanted with *Heuchera* 'Obsidian' makes a stunning centrepiece to this group of pots planted with *Erica carnea*, *Carex testacea*, *Heuchera* 'Plum Pudding' and *Helleborus* × *hybridus*.

choose heucheras. They are excellent in winter containers, particularly the varieties with deep purple foliage, including *Heuchera* 'Licorice'; these look good all year, but the colour of the leaves is even more intense in winter.

## Conifers and heathers

The thought of a dwarf conifer in a pot may conjure an image of *Chamaecyparis lawsoniana* 'Ellwood's Gold' planted in the middle of a plastic Grecian urn. If that puts you off, then try to overcome your aversion to conifers and take a closer look at their diversity of form, colour and texture, which really comes into its own during the winter months. Small specimens can be used as seasonal patio plants, while larger, truly dwarf conifers make excellent long-term subjects for pots.

Winter-flowering heathers, and those with colourful winter foliage, are excellent in containers, either as temporary or permanent subjects. The varieties of *Erica carnea* are most useful for winter flowers because they are more compact. Those with deep pink flowers, such as *Erica carnea* 'Vivellii', work well with purple heucheras and ajugas, while white-flowered ones, including *Erica carnea* 'Springwood White', are good with white-variegated evergreens such as *Euonymus fortunei* 'Emerald Gaiety'. These heathers are lime-tolerant, so they can be grown in any potting compost. Callunas with colourful winter foliage, such as *Calluna vulgaris* 'Robert Chapman', are striking but they need lime-free compost. They make good planting partners for the ground-cover evergreen *Gaultheria procumbens*: with its little white flowers, dark green leaves and large

shining red berries, this is a lovely plant for winter pots. All these heathers will do well in a lightly shaded spot, as well as in full sun.

## Pansies, primroses and polyanthus

Winter pansies and violas always seem the obvious choice for pots after the summer bedding plants have been committed to the compost heap. Pansies need cool night temperatures to initiate flower buds, so it is a mistake to buy and plant them too early. It is also best to buy large cell-grown plants

Above: A riot of tulips – the colour mix changes as later varieties come into bloom. Below: *Cyclamen* Miracle Series can be used outdoors in autumn and early winter.

Once their flowers are over, you can transplant bulbs to the garden, or dispose of them and start again next year. Most bulbs do not perform as well in pots in subsequent years, so it is better to plant new ones than to risk disappointment.

or individually pot-grown ones that are well developed, rather than small, weak ones. Both pansies and violas need a warm, sunny position if they are going to produce flowers during winter and early spring. In a damp shady situation their leaves get spotty, and they look more like seaweed than ornamental garden plants. Pansies need regular dead-heading to keep them flowering well.

Colourful primroses, varieties of *Primula vulgaris,* are produced in their millions for sale early in the new year. Bright and cheerful, they are harbingers of spring and just about irresistible to lift the spirits on those dull days. It is important to remember that they will have been raised in a greenhouse or tunnel and will not take kindly to being planted out in a cold, exposed garden. However, they are ideal to

brighten up a pot in a covered porch or for a really sheltered spot near the house. They come in a wide range of colours: for maximum impact, restrict your colour palette rather than choosing one plant of every shade available.

Some varieties, including *Primula* Husky Series and *Primula* 'Wanda', are hardier and more weather-resistant than others. Young plants can be planted in autumn to flower the following spring, either in sun or in partial shade. Polyanthus, which produce a number of flowers on a single stalk, are also hardy and are normally treated in the same way.

## Cyclamen

Mini cyclamen, especially *Cyclamen* Miracle Series, have become very popular for patio containers. Their graceful flowers are often fragrant and they start to bloom in autumn, continuing through to Christmas. They are damaged by severe frost and rarely perform beyond midwinter. They should be considered as temporary decorations in containers for the first part of the season, to be replaced with primroses or pots of ready-grown spring-flowering bulbs.

## Spring-flowering bulbs

Spring-flowering bulbs provide reliable colour in pots, and will perform at any time from late winter to late spring, depending on what you choose. Growing bulbs in pots, as opposed to planting in the open ground, has many advantages. Bulbs grown in this way are displayed for maximum impact: pots raise bulbs above other planting, so you see them more easily. Smaller-flowering subjects, such as dwarf iris and *Anemone blanda,* can get lost in a garden, particularly if only a few are planted. Growing them in a pot keeps them safe and shows them off to best effect.

It is easy to forget where you have planted bulbs in the open ground, and many are lost by careless cultivation during the winter months. There is no risk of this happening when you grow bulbs in pots. What's more, you do not have to suffer the declining leaves after flowering. Instead you can just remove the pots to a quiet corner of the garden to allow those leaves to die off in peace.

## Growing bulbs with other plants

You can combine flower bulbs and seasonal bedding plants in the same container. It is usually better to group taller bulbs in the middle, and keep lower-growing subjects such as violas, pansies and primroses around the edge. If you spread both over the whole planting area, you often find that the bulbs smother the bedding plants as they grow.

Small bulbs such as species crocus, dwarf irises and the tiniest dwarf narcissi are useful to add early colour, either around the edge of pots or across the centre, before the taller, later bulbs get going.

## Planting in layers

You can keep a pot of bulbs flowering for several weeks by growing more than one variety in the pot, and planting in layers. For this you need a traditional, deep flowerpot at least 30cm (12in) in diameter.

Place a 20cm (8in) layer of multi-purpose compost in the bottom of the pot, then space

the latest-flowering of the bulb varieties you have chosen over the compost, leaving 2cm (¾in) between the bulbs. Tall, late-flowering tulips such as *Tulipa* 'Purissima' or *Tulipa* 'Barbados' would be ideal here.

Next, add a little more compost so that the bottom layer of bulbs is almost covered. Place the next layer between the noses of the bulbs on the bottom layer. For this middle layer, short early tulips such as *Tulipa* 'Red Riding Hood' and *Tulipa* 'Peach Blossom' or narcissi such as 'Hawera' or 'Jack Snipe' would be suitable.

Add more compost, and then add the final layer of bulbs: crocus, muscari, chionodoxa or dwarf iris would be perfect for this. Cover with at least 3cm (1in) of compost and keep moist. This will give a succession of blooms as each layer of bulbs emerges and flowers in turn.

**Top left:** *Anemone blanda* displayed in a shallow bowl. **Above left:** *Crocus sieberi* subsp. *sublimis* 'Tricolor' add colour to the edge of a pot. **Above:** Exotic *Tulipa* 'Barbados' share an urn with dainty jonquils. **Below:** *Tulipa* 'Red Riding Hood' will take over from the muscari in this layered planting.

# A few of the best spring bulbs for pots

Just about any spring-flowering bulbs can be grown in pots – but there are some that are best avoided. Most alliums are not a good idea because their foliage starts to fade when the flowers develop. Some tall double tulips and parrot tulips can be rather floppy and could need some sort of support, which adds to the workload. The leaves of larger daffodils and narcissi can be overpowering and untidy. If you do grow tall bulbs, choose deep pots that are in proportion to the height of the bulbs.

What you really want are good, reliable varieties that need little attention, and have attractive foliage and long-lasting flowers. Here are a few recommendations. Many will perform happily in either sun or light shade, although the tulips and the iris must have a sunny position if they are to flower well.

## For reliable colour

### 1 Narcissus 'Tête-à-Tête'

This has long been the most popular narcissus for pots, and deservedly so. The foliage is bright green and upright, and the clear yellow flowers are daintily poised on strong 15cm (6in) stems. There are usually one, two or three heads on a stem, hence the name. This is a reliable and early narcissus that makes a great planting partner for blue *Anemone blanda*.

2 *Tulipa* 'Red Riding Hood'
Sometimes the old favourites are the best and *Tulipa* 'Red Riding Hood' is one of these. This dwarf tulip has handsome soft green leaves veined with chocolate brown. The foliage is attractive from the time it emerges and is the perfect setting for the elegantly pointed scarlet blooms, carried on 20cm (8in) stems in mid-spring.

### 3 Tulipa tarda

This is a cheery little species tulip for a shallow bowl. The narrow green leaves grow almost horizontally, and in sunny weather the starry white and yellow flowers open flat, just above the leaves. It is an inexpensive bulb to buy, so plant it generously for a pan of pure sunshine on the patio. It flowers in mid-spring.

### 4 Tulipa 'World's Favourite'

There are many Darwin hybrid tulips, all wonderful subjects for medium to large pots. *Tulipa* 'World's Favourite' is perfect if you want a blast of strong colour to waken the garden. The glowing orange blooms are delicately edged with gold. It grows to 40cm (16in) high and flowers in mid-spring.

## For something more sophisticated

### 5 Fritillaria meleagris

The flowers of the snake's head fritillary are exquisite and can be seen to full advantage when grown in a pot. Appearing in mid-spring, they are chequered and lantern-like and come in various shades of purple, or sometimes white; they are carried on slender stems that grow to 20cm (8in) in height. Fritillarias like to be planted as soon as the bulbs are available in early autumn.

They are suitable for small pots providing that you never let them dry out.

## 6 *Iris* 'Katharine Hodgkin'

Perhaps the most intriguingly beautiful of the dwarf irises, 'Katharine Hodgkin' has pale watery blue flowers, marked with yellow and veined in dark blue; these appear at any time from late winter into early spring. It grows to only 10cm (4in), with fine grass-like foliage. Planted in the garden after flowering, it will normally spread and bloom year after year.

## 7 *Narcissus* 'Bell Song'

This elegant and beautiful narcissus has soft cream petals and a short, pale salmon cup. The foliage and flower stems are slender and grow to 30cm (12in) high. Flowering in early to mid-spring, it is lovely in terracotta pots and with blue forget-me-nots.

## 8 *Tulipa* 'Prinses Irene'

This is simply the best tulip for pots. It grows to 30cm (12in) high and has stout stems carrying soft orange flowers delicately flamed with pale mauve and grey. The

blooms open in mid-spring, lasting for three weeks, and the foliage is a delightful blue-grey. If you grow only one flower bulb, grow this.

## 9 *Tulipa saxatilis* Bakeri Group 'Lilac Wonder'

This is a species-type tulip, with narrow shiny green leaves and 20cm (8in) stems carrying silky lilac-pink flowers with bright yellow centres. It is a cheerful and unusual subject for a pot, lovely with purple heucheras in mid-spring.

## For something scented

## 10 *Hyacinthus orientalis* 'Blue Jacket'

Hyacinths are wonderful planted in pots near a doorway, so that you can enjoy their rich scent on the cool spring air. Single hyacinths last longer than double ones and stay upright. 'Blue Jacket' is an excellent choice, with sapphire flowers growing to 20cm (8in) in

height. Smaller bulbs produce smaller flowers, which are less likely to flop over.

## 11 *Muscari macrocarpum* 'Golden Fragrance'

This is a very different grape hyacinth, with tubular soft yellow flowers tinged with purple-brown, on large spikes that grow up to 10cm (4in) high. It blooms in late spring. The plant is slightly tender, so a sunny situation near the house is ideal – and will also allow you to enjoy the fruity fragrance of the flowers as you pass by.

## 12 *Narcissus* 'Bridal Crown'

This is the narcissus for fragrance. In mid- to late spring, each stout 30cm (12in) stem carries two or three sweetly scented, rounded double flowers with creamy petals, flushed gold with a hint of egg yolk in the centre.

See also *Pots: Grasses, ferns and bamboos*, pages 138–139.

# Putting it all together

Here are a few simple plant combinations that work on virtually any soil type. If you use one of each shrub from a collection, and plant them about 90cm (3ft) apart, they should fill a piece of ground up to 2m (6ft) by 3m (10ft), allowing room for some infill planting of bulbs and ground-cover perennials. For a smaller space, you could choose just three or four plants from one of the selections. To fill a longer border, you could simply repeat a selection as necessary; or, for a larger area, you could bulk up the planting by growing the smaller subjects in multiples of three.

Each collection includes an idea for a permanently planted pot. This will provide a focal point, as well as the opportunity to plant around it with shorter plants and bulbs. If the bed or border is beside a path or patio, you could put the pot on the edge of the paving; if not, you could set it on a small area of gravel or paving within the planting. If you do not like the idea of a container, you could grow the plant directly in the ground.

All plants are chosen for ease of cultivation and maintenance. Many are from the main plant selections earlier in the book. These are supplemented with other 'good doers', all brilliant mixers.

## A yellow scheme for sun or partial shade

Golden yellow variegation and soft yellow leaves always attract attention in any part of the garden and they will brighten the darkest corner.

*Osmanthus heterophyllus* **'Goshiki' (1)** has spiky, holly-like evergreen leaves and its diffused creamy-yellow variegation softens stronger yellow foliage. The tiny gold-edged, dark evergreen leaves of *Euonymus japonicus* 'Microphyllus Pulchellus' have a similar effect.

*Lonicera nitida* **'Baggesen's Gold' (2)** has a graceful habit with its softly arching stems

The large-leaved *Hedera colchica* 'Sulphur Heart' with *Euonymus fortunei* 'Emerald 'n' Gold', which, with support, will grow as a climber.

and tiny yellow-green leaves that become more golden in winter, just when you could do with a shot of colour in the garden. *Lonicera nitida* 'Lemon Beauty' has a stiffer habit, but with green leaves edged with gold. Both mix well with more boldly golden variegations, and plants with larger leaves.

*Euonymus japonicus* **'Chollipo' (3)** is a bright golden yellow variegated evergreen of upright habit. It has similar colouring to *Euonymus fortunei* 'Emerald 'n' Gold' (see below) but its larger leaves and taller stature make it the dominant plant in this combination. Alternatively you could use a variegated elaeagnus. The widely planted *Elaeagnus*

### Medium-sized
*Euonymus fortunei* 'Emerald 'n' Gold' (or *Ilex crenata* 'Golden Gem')

*Mahonia aquifolium* 'Apollo' (or *Helleborus* × *hybridus* yellow-flowered)

### Larger
*Euonymus japonicus* 'Chollipo' (or *Elaeagnus pungens* 'Frederici')

*Lonicera nitida* 'Baggesen's Gold' (or *Lonicera nitida* 'Lemon Beauty')

*Osmanthus heterophyllus* 'Goshiki' (or *Euonymus japonicus* 'Microphyllus Pulchellus')

### Fillers
*Ajuga reptans* 'Atropurpurea'

*Crocus chrysanthus* 'E.A. Bowles'

*Vinca minor* 'Illumination'

### For a pot
*Hosta* 'June' (or *Carex oshimensis* 'Evergold')

### Climber for a wall or fence
*Hedera colchica* 'Sulphur Heart'

*pungens* 'Maculata' is similar in colour, but it is rather spreading in habit and tends to produce plain green shoots. *Elaeagnus pungens* 'Frederici' would be a better choice: it has a more compact habit and softer colouring. The narrow evergreen leaves are mainly yellow with a green border.

**Euonymus fortunei 'Emerald 'n' Gold' (4)** has such a strong golden variegation to its dark green evergreen leaves that it stands out wherever it is planted. The Japanese holly *Ilex crenata* 'Golden Gem' is equally striking, but has clear yellow leaves that become greener as they age. It has a stiff, compact, horizontally branched habit.

**Mahonia aquifolium 'Apollo' (6)** is a low, suckering shrub with dark green holly-like leaves that often turn purple-brown in winter. Clusters of yellow flowers appear at the tips of the branches in early spring. This mahonia rarely reaches more than 60cm (2ft) in height, but one plant can spread to cover an area 90cm (3ft) in diameter. A yellow form of *Helleborus* × *hybridus*

would be another option. Although it is an herbaceous perennial, its foliage is almost evergreen and is of a similar colour and texture to that of the mahonia.

A good choice for a pot would be **Hosta 'June' (5)**. The blue-green leaves, gently marked with soft yellow, remain in good condition throughout summer and into early autumn. For winter interest this pot could be changed for one containing the golden yellow *Carex oshimensis* 'Evergold'. This looks lovely in a container because its grass-like foliage drapes gently over the edge of the pot.

For underplanting and ground cover, **Vinca minor 'Illumination' (7)** ensures that the colour theme continues throughout the year. The fine trailing stems carry striking golden yellow leaves edged with dark green.

For contrast, plant **Ajuga reptans 'Atropurpurea' (8)**. Its shining dark purple leaves reflect the winter colour of the mahonia foliage, and its blue spring flowers should coincide with those of the vinca. A few yellow crocus,

such as **Crocus chrysanthus 'E.A. Bowles' (9)**, and dwarf golden yellow narcissi will complete the picture.

When this combination is planted against a fence or wall,

*Hedera colchica* 'Sulphur Heart' (see opposite) makes the perfect backdrop. This ivy has large, dark green shining leaves marked with paler green and boldly splashed yellow.

# A simple green and white planting for shade

**(10)**

Textural foliage and brightly variegated leaves lighten a shady corner. The shrubs in this collection are all evergreen, so it will look good throughout the year.

*Viburnum davidii* (1) is a mainstay in any shady situation, even under the canopy of mature trees. Its large red-stalked, dark green leaves are a striking contrast to the smaller shiny or variegated leaves of other plants in this combination. Alternatively you could choose × *Fatshedera lizei*, with its shining dark green, hand-shaped leaves. Its tall, lax stems are almost climbing, but left to grow as a free-standing shrub it forms a relaxed mound. It is an excellent plant for heavy shade, and deserves to be planted more widely; look out for variegated forms.

*Viburnum tinus* 'Eve Price' (2) is the most popular cultivar of our most widely planted evergreen shrub. It is as tolerant and reliable as *Viburnum davidii*, and its dark green foliage makes a handsome background for the pink buds and rose-tinted flower clusters that grace the plant for several months in winter and early spring. You could use *Choisya ternata* instead. The Mexican orange blossom has shiny emerald-green leaves and scented white flowers in spring or autumn, even when grown in shade.

Nothing delivers fragrance more rewardingly than the unassuming Christmas box, with its tiny pinkish-white flowers in midwinter. *Sarcococca confusa* (3) has upright stems and small, shiny green leaves. *Sarcococca hookeriana* var. *humilis* is similar but has darker green, slightly broader leaves.

*Skimmia × confusa* 'Kew Green' (4) does not produce the red berries or flower buds for which skimmias are generally known. Instead, this compact, dome-shaped shrub has attractive whorls of mid-green leaves, the perfect setting for the yellow-green flower buds that appear in winter; in spring these open to conical heads of yellow-green, deliciously scented flowers. In this combination another option would be *Osmanthus heterophyllus* 'Variegatus', an evergreen of similar proportions to the skimmia, with small dark green, holly-like leaves edged with creamy white.

*Euonymus fortunei* 'Silver Queen' (6) will grow as a short climber or it will form a spreading mound of green and cream variegated leaves. *Euonymus fortunei* 'Emerald Gaiety' is similar but with a whiter variegation and narrower margins on the leaves. Both would work here, but the softer cream variegation of 'Silver Queen' would be more pleasing with *Hedera colchica* 'Dentata Variegata' if this were used as a backdrop. This excellent ivy has large green leaves broadly edged with rich cream.

For a pot, the variegated box *Buxus sempervirens* 'Elegantissima' (5) would make a good choice because of its compact habit and its tiny green, cream-edged leaves. *Euonymus japonicus* 'Microphyllus Albovariegatus' gives a similar effect, but is usually less expensive to buy

## Medium-sized
*Euonymus fortunei* 'Silver Queen' (or *Euonymus fortunei* 'Emerald Gaiety')

*Sarcococca confusa* (or *Sarcococca hookeriana* var. *humilis*)

## Larger
*Skimmia × confusa* 'Kew Green' (or *Osmanthus heterophyllus* 'Variegatus')

*Viburnum davidii* (or × *Fatshedera lizei*)

*Viburnum tinus* 'Eve Price' (or *Choisya ternata*)

## Fillers
*Chionodoxa forbesii*
*Galanthus nivalis*
*Narcissus* 'Jack Snipe'
*Pulmonaria* 'Lewis Palmer'

## For a pot
*Buxus sempervirens* 'Elegantissima' (or *Euonymus japonicus* 'Microphyllus Albovariegatus')

## Climber for a wall or fence
*Hedera colchica* 'Dentata Variegata'

as a mature plant. Both shrubs need little attention and are drought-tolerant.

Spring-flowering bulbs and perennials add early colour. Pulmonarias are robust alternatives to hostas and have the bonus of colourful early flowers. *Pulmonaria* **'Lewis Palmer'** (7) has bright blue flowers in early spring, coinciding with the delightful *Chionodoxa forbesii* (9), whose starry blue and white blooms follow the snowdrops (*Galanthus nivalis*). The spring picture is completed with *Narcissus* **'Jack Snipe'** (8), which has white petals and primrose-yellow trumpets. For later summer colour you could add a pot of white impatiens or begonias.

## Add a hint of pink

In a more open situation, in sun or partial shade, you could add a hint of pink by including any of the following shrubs in the planting scheme.

*Pittosporum tenuifolium* 'Elizabeth' has a light habit and small green and white leaves that are tinged with pink, especially in winter.

It could be used as an alternative to *Viburnum tinus* 'Eve Price'. In a sunny site, *Euonymus fortunei* 'Emerald Gaiety' and 'Silver Queen' also become tinged pink in winter; either would work well with the pittosporum or with the viburnum.

*Cornus alba* **'Sibirica Variegata'** (10) would add red stems in winter and larger green and white variegated leaves in summer. These are also flushed with deep pink, especially in autumn. As it is deciduous, the planting picture would change with the seasons, which might provide additional interest.

With its domed, compact habit, *Hebe* 'Red Edge' would be an alternative to *Skimmia* × *confusa* 'Kew Green'. Its neat grey-green foliage, edged with purple-red in winter, stands out against the dark leaves of *Viburnum davidii*, which looks just as good in a sunny spot as it does in shade.

The pink notes in these plants would work especially well with purple foliage. You could add *Berberis thunbergii* f. *atropurpurea* 'Rose Glow', perhaps in place of the sarcococca. Alternatively,

you could use *Heuchera* 'Plum Pudding' instead of the pulmonaria. The large pinkish-purple, wavy-edged leaves of this heuchera remain in fine condition throughout the year.

For a pot, a dramatic dark phormium would be excellent. *Phormium* 'Platt's Black' has deep purple-black leaves that arch gently and have more movement than many phormiums.

# Year-round interest in a sunny situation

10

Silver foliage and aromatic leaves combine with bright summer blooms in this drought-tolerant selection for a sun-drenched border on well-drained soil. Dwarf tulips and alliums add spring and early summer colour year after year. The dark leaves of the pittosporum and heuchera add depth and contrast.

Cistus are excellent evergreen shrubs for sunny, well-drained positions. Most varieties dislike pruning and can become rather straggly with age. **Cistus × pulverulentus 'Sunset'** (1) is one of the best, with its soft felty foliage, compact, tidy habit and bright purple-pink flowers produced over a long period from early summer. If you do not like the idea of bright pink, substitute with *Cistus × obtusifolius* 'Thrive', which has profuse white flowers and small dark green leaves; alternatively, use the hardy and reliable *Potentilla fruticosa* 'Primrose Beauty', with fine grey-green foliage and soft yellow buttercup-like flowers. The potentilla loses its leaves in winter, but makes up for it by never being out of bloom through summer and autumn.

Aromatics flourish in hot, dry situations: thyme, rosemary, sage, curry plant (*Helichrysum*) and cotton lavender (*Santolina*) are all Mediterranean natives, so they dislike wet conditions and thrive in drought. Silver foliage lifts any planting combination in sun, and it mixes wonderfully with both soft and bright colours. Santolina has finely divided silver-green foliage on a shrub with a softly rounded habit. The pale creamy-yellow midsummer flowers of *Santolina pinnata* **subsp.** *neapolitana* (2) will come as a pleasant surprise if you are familiar with the violent mustard blooms of *Santolina chamaecyparissus*. Another option is *Helichrysum italicum* 'Korma', which has narrow leaves of the brightest silver that stay looking good throughout the winter. Creamy flowers on silver stems appear from midsummer. It makes a superb backdrop for the silvery lilac flowers of **Allium cristophii** (9) in late spring and early summer, and hides the allium's ugly foliage.

Sedums have grey-green succulent foliage on stout stems, and the texture is a pleasing contrast to the lighter, more feathery foliage of the silver-leaved plants. The flat pink flowerheads of **Sedum 'Herbstfreude'** (3), borne in late summer and early autumn, are a magnet for bees and other pollinating insects. The sedum's gentle colours mean that it will sit easily alongside the softly hued foliage and brightly coloured blooms of its neighbours in this scheme. Also attractive to insects are the spikes of rich blue flowers produced in midsummer by the purple sage, *Salvia officinalis* 'Purpurascens'. With its soft mauve-grey foliage, which forms a gently undulating mound, this too is a wonderful mixer.

---

**Low**

*Berberis thunbergii* 'Admiration' (or *Helianthemum* 'Cerise Queen')

*Heuchera* 'Licorice'

*Lavandula angustifolia* 'Hidcote' (or *Lavandula pedunculata* subsp. *pedunculata*, known as *Lavandula stoechas* 'Papillon')

**Medium-sized**

*Cistus × pulverulentus* 'Sunset' (or *Cistus × obtusifolius* 'Thrive' or *Potentilla fruticosa* 'Primrose Beauty')

*Santolina pinnata* subsp. *neapolitana* (or *Helichrysum italicum* 'Korma')

*Sedum* 'Herbstfreude' (or *Salvia officinalis* 'Purpurascens')

**Fillers**

*Allium cristophii*

*Cyclamen coum*

*Tulipa saxatilis* Bakeri Group 'Lilac Wonder'

**For a pot**

*Pittosporum tenuifolium* 'Tom Thumb' (or *Phormium* 'Sundowner')

The blue lavenders make excellent planting partners for any of these shrubs. The ever-popular *Lavandula angustifolia* 'Hidcote' (**4**) has deep blue flowers carried above silver foliage. Not so hardy and reliable but one of the showiest lavenders, *Lavandula stoechas* 'Papillon' produces its winged bluish-purple flowerheads from early summer to autumn. It has an upright habit and grey-green evergreen leaves. An annual trim after flowering is the only maintenance that these lavenders require.

Although it has no flowers to speak of, *Berberis thunbergii* 'Admiration' (**6**) provides colour and interest over a long period with its wonderful red-purple, gold-edged foliage and fabulous autumn colour. It is a tiny and compact shrub and needs no maintenance. As an alternative, you could choose one of the sun roses (*Helianthemum*). These are great performers in early summer and are suitable for the smallest of sunny gardens. Their double or single flowers are produced in great profusion on low,

spreading plants with shining evergreen or grey-green foliage. To keep sun roses in shape, trim them back after flowering, to a point just beneath where the flower stalks arise. *Helianthemum* 'Cerise Queen' is a lovely double variety with layers of cerise petals and golden stamens.

For a focal point in a pot you could add another soft shape in the form of *Pittosporum tenuifolium* 'Tom Thumb' (**5**), with its shining purple-black evergreen foliage, or you may like the contrast provided by the spiky *Phormium* 'Sundowner', with its bright and beautiful bronze-green leaves margined with deep pink.

The gently waved leaves of dark purple *Heuchera* 'Licorice' (**10**) complete the picture, together with the silver-green foliage and sugar-pink flowers of *Cyclamen coum* (**7**) in late winter. In spring the silky lilac-pink, yellow-centred flowers of *Tulipa saxatilis* Bakeri Group 'Lilac Wonder' (**8**) are very eyecatching and an appropriate forerunner to the cistus flowers.

Silver foliage shrubs and sun-lovers such as helianthemums and cistus sit well beside paving and areas of gravel or scree planted with thymes and sedums (see pages 20–23). The result is a low-maintenance planting that looks good all year; it also copes with periods of winter wet, providing the soil is well drained. Add a spiky phormium, cordyline or yucca for height and contrast. Other good shrubs for similar conditions are *Ballota pseudodictamnus*, *Genista lydia*, *Lotus hirsutus* and *Prostanthera cuneata*.

# A last word

Whatever stage you are at in your gardening life remember that no garden stands still: you plant it, it grows and matures, and at some point it needs rejuvenation.

Just because you have put thought and planning into your plot, perhaps with many years of gardening experience behind you, it does not mean that you will get everything right all of the time. One of those carefully selected shrubs will not have read the text book and will grow way beyond its designated proportions, or it will sulk and remain a midget.

Be prepared to change your mind: if the planting does not look as you want it to, make alterations. If you really do not like a plant, or it fails to perform, dig it up and give it to a friend, or consign it to the compost heap.

If you allow your garden to sink into decline, and it does not please you when you look out of the window, then you really have lost the plot. Never give up: just change your approach to gardening to suit the time in your life.

# Index

## *Credits*

Andrew McIndoe and AA Publishing would like to thank all those whose gardens feature in this book.

All photographs were taken by Andrew McIndoe except those listed below.

20(3) GAP Photos/John Glover;  20(6) GAP Photos/Visions;  21(7) GAP Photos/Pernilla Bergdahl;  21(9) GAP Photos/John Glover;  21(10) GAP Photos/Richard Bloom;  22(13) GAP Photos/Amanda Darcy;  23a GAP Photos/JS Sira;  23c GAP Photos/Howard Rice;  24b GAP Photos/Maxine Adcock;  25b GAP Photos/Zara Napier;  27a GAP Photos/JS Sira;  28a GAP Photos/Janet Johnson;  29 GAP Photos/Lynn Keddie;  33(9) Kevin Hobbs;  34 GAP Photos/Mark Bolton (Design: Sheila White);  35b GAP Photos/Jerry Harpur (Design: Tom Stuart Smith);  36 GAP Photos/Elke Borkowski;  38b Forest Garden Products;  41 Robin Whitecross;  49 GAP Photos/Elke Borkowski (Jahnke Garden);  50(1) David Austin Roses;  50(4) GAP Photos/Jerry Harpur;  50(5) GAP Photos/John Glover;  51a GAP Photos/Mark Bolton;  51(7) GAP Photos/Rob Whitworth (Design: Beccy Pook);  51(8) GAP Photos/Mel Watson;  56a Robin Whitecross;  57c Robin Whitecross;  61(1) GAP Photos/Visions;  61(2) GAP Photos/JS Sira;  61(3) GAP Photos/Carole Drake;  61(4) GAP Photos/Elke Borkowski;  62a GAP Photos/Clive Nichols (Design: Malley Terry);  63 GAP Photos/Juliette Wade;  69b Robin Whitecross;  70a GAP Photos/Jerry Harpur;  71a GAP Photos/S & O;  71b GAP Photos/Jerry Harpur;  71c GAP Photos/Howard Rice;  72a GAP Photos/Dianna Jazwinski;  72b GAP Photos/Juliette Wade;  73a GAP Photos/Mel Watson;  73b GAP Photos/Suzie Gibbons;  73c GAP Photos/John Glover;  83(4) GAP Photos/Marcus Harpur;  84(9) GAP Photos/Friedrich Strauss;  85(11) GAP Photos/Neil Holmes;  87b GAP Photos/John Glover;  92(9) GAP Photos/Zara Napier;  93(10) GAP Photos/Carole Drake;  95(8) Osberton Nurseries;  103(11) GAP Photos/Michael Howes;  104b David Austin Roses;  106 David Austin Roses;  107 David Austin Roses;  113a Pip Bensley;  114b New Leaf Plants;  115b Pip Bensley;  116(9) David Austin Roses;  123(10) GAP Photos/Howard Rice;  126(2) Robin Whitecross;  127(9) GAP Photos/S & O;  134a Charlotte Strutt;  139d Sue Gordon;  145 GAP Photos/Richard Bloom;  153(4) GAP Photos/Carole Drake

| LE | 6/09 |
|---|---|
|  |  |
|  |  |
|  |  |
|  |  |
|  |  |
|  |  |
|  |  |
|  |  |
|  |  |